"The Truth WILL out."
-Jam'all Mokolo

How Tithing Killed My Mom

A Guide to Guilt-FREE Giving

By Jam'all Mokolo

Copyright © 2023 by Jam'all Mokolo

All rights reserved. This book or any portion thereof may not be reproduced or used in any manner whatsoever without the express written permission of the publisher except for the use of brief quotations in a book review.

Black Seeds Publishing
911 Carr Avenue
Clarksdale, Mississippi 38614
www.blackseedspublishing.com

Unless otherwise noted, Scripture taken from the Holy Bible, NEW INTERNATIONAL VERSION®, NIV® Copyright © 1973, 1978, 1984, 2011 by Biblica, Inc.® Used by permission. All rights reserved worldwide.

Scripture quotations taken from the Holy Bible, King James Version.

Taken from the Complete Jewish Bible by David H. Stern. Copyright © 1998. All rights reserved. Used by permission of Messianic Jewish Publishers, 6120 Day Long Lane, Clarksville, MD 21029. www.messianicjewish.net.

References from the Jewish Encyclopedia, 2002-2021, https://www.jewishencyclopedia.com/ and the 618 Jewish Laws or MITZVOT

Printed in the United States of America

ISBN-13: 979-8-9878956-0-3

"If the truth kills them - let them die."
—Ayn Rand, 20th Century Philosopher

It basically means, "If your beliefs about something or someone are wrong, it's better to discover this sooner than later."
—Jam'all Mokolo

~ Dedication & Acknowledgment ~

This book is dedicated to my mom, who had nothing yet gave everything.

I would also like to thank her for giving me the inspiration to write the book, through our real life experiences, that today allows me to share with readers in the hopes that they will better understand the true meaning of tithing, and that it's no longer a command for us today.

It is not a book against tithing, it's a book that's *for giving*, and no one gave more than my mom—yet died with nothing to show for it.

It is my strong opinion that the misunderstanding of tithes, tithing, and the biblical tithe, is being misapplied to today's times, and has contributed to making the poor poorer, while making the Christian rich *richer*.

My intent is to point out how proportionate and New Testament giving will allow the Moms of today to prosper, and keep on living fearlessly, scripturally, and guilt-free!

My main research came from "The King James Bible, the Complete Jewish Bible, the Jewish Encyclopedia, the 618 Jewish Laws, and the most important tool "My Life".

"It is the duty of every man, as far as his ability extends, to detect and expose delusion and error."
—Thomas Paine

~Table of Contents~

Chapter 1
Will a Pastor Rob a Single Mom? 1

Chapter 2
How a Mom Couldn't Rob God 5

Chapter 3
How my Mom Confused the 'Storehouse' With a 'Bank Account' 10

Chapter 4
How my Mom Thought 'Flipture' Was Scripture 15

Chapter 5
How my Mom Thought 'Tithe of the Land' Meant 'Tithe From the Hand' 22

Chapter 6
How my Mom Thought 'Blessings Could Be Bought' 30

Chapter 7
How my Mom Thought 'Wanting' Means 'Getting' 37

Chapter 8
How my Mom Thought Trusting in a Pastor, Was 'Trusting in God' 41

Chapter 9
How a Mom Can Sometimes Chose 'Me-Search' Over Research 46

Chapter 10
How a Mom Can Study To Find Herself 'Confused' 51

Chapter 11
How a Mom That's a Tither, Can Really Be a 'Lie-Ther' 61

Chapter 12
'The Truth in Love' Conversation About Tithing for Moms (and Pastors) 65

Chapter 13
How a Mom Can Be Set Free, To Live Stress Free 107

Chapter 14
How Belief Can 'Kill' a Mom 112

Chapter 15
How a Mom Can See Observation, as 'Wisdom' 120

Chapter 16
How a Mom Can Fast From 'Tithing' 125

Chapter 17
How a Mom Is Honored 'With Truth' 136

Chapter 18
A Guide for Guilt-Free Giving 139

Chapter 19
10 Reasons Christians Struggle With 'Tithing Guilt'........143

Chapter 20
10 Steps To Be Guilt-Free From Tithing for Good............147

Chapter 21
10 Things my Mom Never Received From Biblical Tithing 153

Chapter 22
Channel Your Pain To Take Action! 157

About the Author 160

How Tithing Killed My Mom

A Guide to Guilt-FREE Giving

By Jam'all Mokolo

Chapter 1

Will a Pastor Rob a Single Mom?

"Will a man rob a single mom?" —Mala**lie** 1:1

Absolutely and it happens somewhere every Sunday!

[Singing] "Money, Money, Money, Money... MONEY!" 🎵🎵🎵

That hit song from the 70s blasts loudly in my mind whenever I hear a pastor ask for tithes in today's church. But, in reality, the music preceding the pastor's

Chapter 1

announcement that it was time to tithe was less like the joy that came from the hook of the song "Money".

Instead, it was more like the sadness of a funeral song for the sudden death of your purse... I know from experience that for my mom, tithes and offering time became "tithes and suffering time." It was because it reminded her of what she did not have.

For others, it was the moment they suddenly have to lift that finger to go to the ladies' room while the ushers block the exits or that moment they ball up their money to toss it into the offering plate (so their neighbor doesn't see that it was only two dollar bills).

For some—like me—it's that moment that knocks the air out of your stomach, like a punch from a big sister protecting her little sister that you made cry from calling her a 'meatball head'. Or, it's a reminder that giving her last two dollars out of faith meant hitching a ride, borrowing bus fare from a member, or even worse, walking home—which was about four miles. These four miles might as well have been 15 miles for her four children and only one of the many reminders of the unnecessary suffering we had to endure.

Join me, if you will, as I share my personal journey of over 20 years of experience with a tithing woman, and if there

Single Moms vs Pastors

ever was an example of living, believing, or tithing by faith, it was her. That person of faith was my mom.

- $ $ $ -

"Yes sir!" Pastor Feel-Good sure delivered a fast food buffet of a message today, and then at the end of his "bait, manipulate, and switch" sermon, I realized he had a pattern. His sermons always seemed to parallel tithing. I mean, *really*? If the message was "Jesus Wept," it somehow would end up being because his sheeple weren't tithing.

- $ $ $ -

Once, I remember a pastor striking fear in the congregation's hearts by calling ALL the children up to the altar, then blasphemously saying,

> "Parents, look at your children... aren't they beautiful? You love them, right? Well, God said to give a dollar for every year you want them to live. If you don't give but a few dollars, then it means that you don't want them to live much longer. Amen?!"

I could see the sad faces of those moms who were broke and had nothing to offer but their hearts. I could see that it was killing them that they had nothing to give, and this type of misinterpreted doctrine is slowly killing moms around the world today... as it did mine.

Chapter 1

First, they bait you by sharing the joy of the Word, manipulate you by inducing guilt through their words, then switch the initial message from *giving* you hope to *selling* you hope by requiring the unbiblical tithe.

Tithing under the Jewish law today is outdated, outmoded, and obsolete. Free-will giving is all that is required today to support the gospel, according to the Bible, after the work on the cross was finished.

But we'll get into that later because right now, I want to tell you a little about my mom. For those of you who will question my mother's level of faith with that judgmental mindset some Christians use to feel better about themselves, let me say that:

1) Her faith was second to no one's on the planet, and

2) Everyone's measuring stick for faith is subjective. Some people can afford to stand comfortably in the $1,000 faith offering line; and some are subtly trembling as they stand in the $10 faith offering line because they know it could buy a few days of groceries… that was my mom.

Now, open up your Bibles…

Chapter 2

How a Mom Couldn't Rob God

"Can a person rob God? Yet, you rob me. But you ask, 'How have we robbed you?' In tenths, and voluntary contributions." —Malachi 3:8 [Complete Jewish Bible]

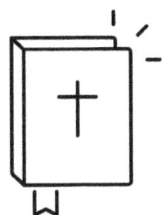

When you read that first part, how did it make you feel?

Did it make you feel scared, nervous, stressed, guilty, or uncomfortable?

I know for my mom, it made her feel all of the above. These feelings can chip away at our mental, physical, and spiritual well-being, eventually killing us. If you felt any or all of

Chapter 2

these same feelings, it could be because you are giving out of compulsion and you haven't studied your Word! (This is the place where a well-studied pastor would say, "Uh oh- it's quiet in here now!")

If you study the text and do the research, then you'd discover that those scriptures weren't talking to you or me. Malachi was addressing the Jewish Nation of that time. If my mom had known this, it might have saved her a lot of unnecessary emotional turmoil and given her the relief that may have prolonged her life well past 57 years.

If she had access to the information available to all of us today, then there's no doubt in my mind that she would have stopped tithing and given differently. However, some pastors choose not to share this truth about tithing because it could cost them their mortgage, Bentley payment, or maybe even their job. If it's going to cost them all those material gifts, then they would rather you not know that you are no longer under the Levitical tithing law!

-$ $ $-

Well, my mom would have wanted to know this fact; however, like many other moms who were indoctrinated into this belief, she chose to tithe on everything from her welfare check to her child support payments. As you can imagine, a single mom with four kids should never be obligated to tithe... she should receive the tithes.

> "Ye are cursed with a curse: for ye have robbed me, even this whole nation." —Malachi 3:9

This scripture was even scarier for my mom. Another interpretation says: "A curse is on you, on your whole Nation, because you rob me."

Like many of you today, she took this verse literally. However, if she had studied the text, it would have been revealed to her that we (me and you) weren't in the room when this was said!

At the entrance of our church was a large drawing of our future church that the tithes were supposed to be building. It was there so that everyone could see our future house of worship! (Ask me if it ever came to fruition?)

That picture displayed there brought lots of "Oohs and Ahhs" whenever people saw it, and even my mother would say, "That sure is going to be nice!"

I said the same thing when I saw the large play area for kids! As I recall, I was a playfully led 11 or 12-year-old, so the playground ministry was my calling at the time!

Chapter 2

My mother also expressed to me during this time that she felt it was her religious duty, Christian obligation, and spiritual responsibility to give everything she could to bring the new building to fruition. In return, God would bless her with the desires of her heart!

So, one day after church, I had the unmitigated gall to ask, "Moma, why do you give your money to the church when sometimes we don't have food for groceries?" By her reaction, you would have thought I had asked her why did she watch the Tom Jones Show after we'd gone to bed!

[Tom Jones had his own ministry that was a night service for ladies only – Google him and you'll know what I mean! :-)]

She looked at me and I could have sworn her head turned backward, like Linda Blair's in the "Exorcist". She said, "Honey, the devil IS a liar! You ain't going to bring no curse on me... talking about why I give my money to the church. Boy, I rebuke you in the NAME of Jesus! Ula-ma-ma cee- la- ma-ma cee- ti!"

Yep! I remember that last phrase like she said it yesterday. That last part was her speaking in tongues, which from the age of 10, often made my eyes water, from biting my bottom lip to keep me from laughing out loud! I mean, where was the interpreter of those tongues?

Can't Rob God

I never laughed out loud though because not only would it be a sign of disrespect that would have earned a slap that sent me into next Sunday, but because I also believed at the time that a curse would come upon my mom because I knew no better back then.

Today, I know better and I wish I could have shared with her **Galatians 3:13**. This Scripture states, **"Christ redeemed us from the curse of the law, by becoming a curse for us, for it is written: Cursed is everyone, who is hung on a pole."**

My mom never read this. I hope yours does because it might save her life and some money. After all, the truth is tithing was—uh oh, watch out now—NEVER money! I can hear Pastor Get-Right saying, "Uh oh…y'all quiet now!"

Now, open up your Lie-bles, to Mala-lie 2:2…

Chapter 3

How my Mom Confused the 'Storehouse' With a 'Bank Account'

"Bring the whole tenth of your income into the storehouse, and put me to the test — and set it next to the fruits, vegetables, and animals." —Malalie 1:2

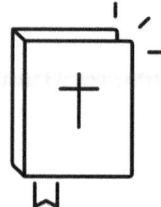

"C'mon boy, let's go over to this welfare office and get some food boxes."

Storehouse vs Bank Account

We were raised in the projects, and my mom received a welfare check on the first of every month. I always knew when it was about to be the first of the month because when my mom had run out of money or food stamps, I'd have to go with her to get government food—cheese, canned meat, canned chicken, and my least favorite, powdered milk. Yuk!

Don't get me wrong, when you're hungry, that government food tasted like a free buffet at Golden Corral on Family Night. However, I believe that if my mom had known that tithing was NEVER money and that the church isn't the storehouse, then she would have had enough of it to make sure that she and her children would never have to eat anything less nutritious than a home-cooked meal.

Unfortunately, we were often forced to submit to a meal that was always a mental, physical, and spiritual reminder to her of how cursed we were according to her understanding of the Word. I believe this is what the Scripture means when it says in **Hosea 4:6, "My people are destroyed for lack of knowledge"** or in our case, are hungry for lack of knowledge!

That said, once you've studied and applied your new knowledge to your life, you know better and do better. Unfortunately, my mom didn't know this in her time; otherwise, I believe she would have lived better.

Chapter 3

- $ $ $ -

You see, my tithe-guilted brethren, there actually was a "storehouse" for food! However, today's pastors associate and conform the storehouse to mean a bank account. You can see how closely they resemble each other, right? Not!

One is for storing agricultural produce and one is for storing money. In your bank, do you store your money next to fruits, vegetables, and cattle? That would be ridiculous, right?!

Well, neither did they back then, and the ONLY time money was an exception was when a man needed to give money as a substitute, of which he was penalized a fifth part added: *"If you want to buy back the Lord's tenth of the grain or fruit, you must pay its value, plus 20%."*

> **"And if a man will at all redeem ought of his tithes, he shall add thereto the fifth part thereof."—Leviticus 27:31**

Or, if you were too far away from the house of worship,

> **"And if the way be too long for thee, so that thou art not able to carry it; or if the place be too far from thee, which the Lord thy God shall choose to set his name there, when the Lord thy God hath blessed thee..."**
> **—Deuteronomy 14: 24, 25**

Storehouse vs Bank Account

If you read **Deuteronomy 14:26**, you will discover the true purpose of this tithe:

"And thou shalt bestow that money for whatsoever thy soul lusteth after, for oxen, or for sheep, or for wine, or for strong drink, or for whatsoever thy soul desireth: and thou shalt eat there before the Lord thy God, and thou shalt rejoice, thou, and thine household..."

"Use the silver to buy whatever you like: cattle, sheep, goats, wine, or other alcoholic drink. Then feast there in the presence of the Lord your God and celebrate with your household." It was a celebration of the Israelites' blessings, including the widowers, the fatherless, and the poor.

Has anyone ever been included in the presence of the elders after service, counted up the money, and then split up the tithes amongst themselves? Not without a quick chop to the throat or an elbow to the eye socket!

- $ $ $ -

So you see, my calorie-depleted brethren, the tithes were actually food! They were edible and allotted for the Levites and Priests. Out of this food in the storehouse, a tithe was given to the Levites, and then a tenth was given to the Levitical priests from the Levites.

Chapter 3

The redundant point I'm trying to make is the storehouse was literally a storehouse, and not your church's bank account. The tithes were something that was consumed, not spent.

The storehouse also held grain, olive oil, and wine, as stated in **2 Chronicles 31: 4 - 11**. Please don't take my word for it. Study it for yourself, and find yourself approved.

While you're at it, tell your mom that she doesn't have to tithe her grocery money either. In all actuality, the tithes were not designed to go towards the church building fund at all; they were to go to the Levite, the foreigner, the fatherless, the poor, and the widowers, according to **Deuteronomy 26:12: "When you have finished laying aside all the tithe of your increase in the third year—the year of tithing—and have given it to the Levite, the stranger, the fatherless, and the widow, so that they may eat within your gates and be filled..."**

Notice it says the third year and not every Sunday.

- $ $ $ -

Truth be told, a portion of the tithes were supposed to go to my mom and her four kids and not towards anyone's car payment, bank account, or building fund.

Chapter 4

How my Mom Thought 'Flipture' Was Scripture

"Give your tithes, and it will be given back to you in good measure, pressed down, shaken together- and a check for $682,000, will also arrive in your mailbox." —Mala**lie** 1:3

The devil is a liar, right? However, my mom interpreted it exactly like the above "flipture." The actual scripture is:

"Give, and it will be given to you. A good measure, pressed down, shaken together and running over, will be

Chapter 4

poured into your lap. For with the measure you use, it will be measured to you." —Luke 6:38 (NIV)

Wouldn't it be great if that scripture was actually talking about material things and money?! Sorry, it's not! It's talking about forgiveness. *I'll let you study that for yourself in its proper context.*

Now, if you have a cell phone, you are familiar with annoying telemarketers trying to sell you something you don't need and keep calling you day and night. Depending upon your mobile carrier, the name "Scam Likely" flashes across the phone screen. Depending on how late they call, this can also cause your significant other to look at you sideways.

Well, I had the displeasure of finally meeting Mr. Scam Likely, and he turned out to be a pastor! His real name was Pastor Robinson, however, I'd like to refer to him unaffectionately as "Pastor Robbing-some"!

It was on a hot, broken air conditioner, fan-fanning Monday night service, that my most memorable moment of "something's not right with this tithing thang" happened.

It was the first night of a week-long revival, and on the last day of the revival, this guest pastor said he was going to

Flipture vs Scripture

reveal who the Antichrist was on a projector screen. He also told our pastor that God said he was going to get that new building for being obedient and allowing him to have the revival there that week. Oh, but the "prophe-lying" didn't end there.

He also said, "God said that anyone who tithed faithfully during this revival, He would open up the windows of Heaven, and send you an increase of 100 times the amount in return in the mail." He then asked the sheeple to form a $1,000 line, a $500 line, a $100 line, and lastly, a "whatever God puts on your heart to give" line.

My mom looked at me and said, "Honey, that man of God just said if I gave what was in my purse, that God was going to send me a check in the mail?! Gimme my purse, Hallelujah! Glory!" My mom gave her last $20 that night, and when the money hit the bottom of the offering plate, I could have sworn the sound triggered the trauma that I could only describe as my hunger pains. If she had studied the text, then she would have discovered what opening the windows of Heaven really was:

> "Bring the whole tithe into the storehouse, that there may be food in my house. Test me in this," says the Lord Almighty, "and see if I will not throw open the floodgates of heaven and pour out so much blessing that there will not be room enough to store it." —Malachi 3:10 (NIV)

Chapter 4

I found that the people of Judah weren't bringing in all the tithes, or holding back some, or not tithing at all. The floodgates that the text is talking about, regarding the windows of Heaven, is rain—not "making it rain" with dollar bills!

Genesis 7: 11,12 talks about how **"the windows of Heaven were opened up, and it rained for 40 days and 40 nights."** How else are you going to fill the storehouse with agriculture if there is no rain to grow the crops? So if you didn't pay your tithing bill, God would cut off your Heavenly water!

How about this: How will you tithe if you don't even have a field? Uh oh! "Reverend Get-Right done made somebody nervous, and somebody else is quiet up in here again! Shumbola- lo- lo!"

Before the shouting music begins, let me finish the story because it gets much, much worse...

- $ $ $ -

My mother was expecting a check in the mail that was coming from a settlement—$682 to be exact. In 1973 that was a lot of money, and I already knew what I wanted to do with the $100 promised to me to buy anything I wanted.

Flipture vs Scripture

Are you serious? One hundred dollars?! I was going to be rich! I had chosen to buy a football game, shoes, and especially clothes because we only had three shirts and pants for the entire school year that I could remember growing up.

So I had been looking through the popular Sears catalog and had picked out three shirt and pants outfits, some shoes from Eleganza magazine (a well-known Black fashion catalog back then), and a Tudor electric football game with all the teams! (I was a football fanatic!)

I would come home from school every day and imagine how I would mix and match my outfits to look like I had six new ones, with my cool shoes that went with all of them, and had started writing a schedule of football games between the teams! I was happier than a tither in good standing! And then, one day, I came home from school and heard the most devastating news a 12-year-old with promised gifts should never, ever hear.

I rushed through the door every day after school in anticipation of hearing that the check had arrived and that everything I had wanted was ordered and on the way! However, I never expected that everything I ever wanted would be taken away like a puff of smoke after my dreams were set on fire with these words:

Chapter 4

"I got the check today, but I gave it to the revival pastor, so we could get $682,000 in the mail! We're going to have everything we ever wanted!" My mom said excitedly.

If I could have seen my face back then, from a parent's perspective, there is no way I could not have seen the disappointment, heartbreak, shock, and disbelief on my child's face—and never forget it.

So likewise, my mom saw the trauma this news created for me at the moment by my reaction of walking away and closing my bedroom door. As I walked away, I saw her joyous smile slowly fade, reflecting a hint of sorrow. It was one of the few times my mom noticed my emotional pain and made it more important than her religious gain.

- $ $ $ -

After that traumatic experience, I would find myself checking our mailbox in the hopes of $682,000 arriving in our mailbox. However, just like expecting Santa Claus to come down the chimney in the housing projects—where there are no chimneys—that's NEVER going to happen.

So I stopped expecting it. My mom, on the other hand, kept on keeping the faith.

To this day, the pastor never got that new building, no one who gave $1,000 received $1,000,000, no one who gave

Flipture vs Scripture

$500 received $500,000, no one who gave $100 received $10,000, and no one who gave $682 received $682,000—and that person, my mom, died waiting for it.

Chapter 5

How my Mom Thought 'Tithe of the Land' Meant 'Tithe From the Hand'

"Every tithe of the herd and flock—every tenth animal that passes under the shepherd's rod—will be holy to the LORD - including your stimulus, income tax, and unemployment check." —Mala**lie** 1:4

Around March 2020, the World Health Organization (WHO) declared coronavirus disease 2019 (COVID-19), caused by

Tithe from the Hand

the severe acute respiratory syndrome coronavirus 2 (SARS COV-2), a global pandemic.

As a result, people lost their loved ones, their businesses, their jobs, their savings, their homes, their marriages, and some even lost their churches.

The government then decided to send out rounds of stimulus checks to help people provide the essential resources on which to live. However, some churches still practice the Old Testament tithing law and required their members to tithe on the monies they need to survive. In other words, that's like expecting you to tithe from the fruit and vegetables that the Levitical temple gave you to feed yourself and your family!

- $ $ $ -

However, no one I know tithed during that time, and you know why? Because they couldn't have, and shouldn't have to, mainly because they didn't own a field, or have a job, to tithe from! The actual text, **Leviticus 27:32** says:

"Every tithe of the herd and flock—every tenth animal that passes under the shepherd's rod—will be holy to the Lord."

Chapter 5

Are you a farmer and owner of a flock? Or do you have ten animals? Then why would you tithe on what you do not have?!

Notice the text said "10" animals because if you only had nine, you weren't required to tithe—which means those without can't tithe. And why? Because they can't afford to. Even God knew you couldn't tithe from what you did not have!

- $ $ $ -

How will you survive without food, water, and shelter—which are your fundamental survival needs—if you tithe with the money that provides those needs?

Leviticus 27:32 is one of many Scriptures that my mom misunderstood. Not only could it have kept me and my siblings well-fed had she understood it correctly, but it also could have eased the guilt she felt when she couldn't give anything but her presence in her church.

If anyone ever tithed her time, it was my mom because even when she didn't have the money or transportation, she found a way to get to church on Monday, Wednesday, and Friday, and stayed for all three services on Sunday. Don't tell me that this woman wasn't a woman of faith!

Tithe from the Hand

We all know the phrase, *How can one give what they do not have?* How could one tithe without a field to grow crops? The simple answer is, "They can't," so those without fields weren't required to!

This was simply because if you didn't have a field, then there was no way you could tithe from the land... "Hello people, is this mic on?!"

Leviticus 27:30 says it even better,

"And all the tithe of the land, whether of the seed of the land or of the fruit of the tree is the Lord's. It is holy to the Lord."

Nowhere in this text does it say to tithe from your income or 'printed money'. Why is that, Reverend Get-Right, you ask? It's because the God of the children of Israel wanted them to tithe from what He created, not from what man created.

Here's a good example:

My mom could make a killer chicken and dumplings meal, and if tithes were killer chicken and dumpling meals, she could easily tithe that by providing the recipe and buying the groceries.

Chapter 5

If she had to produce the actual chicken, she couldn't; she'd have to rely on God for that. If tithes were money, all you would have to do is get a job (or own a money mint), and there would be no need to have faith because you could easily produce it through work.

However, if you had a field, you'd have to rely on the windows of heaven to open to provide the rain, meaning you would have to depend solely on God. My mom giving money as the tithes were like planting a seed in infertile soil because nothing grew from it or manifested personal increase—it only increased the church's bank account.

Now I understand why whenever my mom would go to seek help from her church, they would tell her, "The storehouse is empty, my sister." It's because there never ever was a *real storehouse*, and they knew what she was asking for required a withdrawal slip that they weren't going to provide. The disappointment on her face when she returned from being denied help from her own church had to be killing her, and it eventually did just that.

When the COVID-19 pandemic caused lockdowns all over the entire world, many churches closed down—stopping their ministry flow and the tithing flow. However, that should never stop the Gospel of the Truth.

Tithe from the Hand

The saying goes, *the truth will out*—meaning the truth will always come out. That being said, if your church closes down as a result of non-tithers, then maybe, like a restaurant with an "F" rating, it might have needed to close down. And perhaps because it's not meeting the basic spiritual food requirements to serve the truth, then what might happen is people will find a church where the truth of the message will sustain them through any pandemic, and especially this tithing pandemic.

Some of our pastors, ministers, bishops, prophets, and prophetesses today don't start churches out of a 'calling', an inspiration, or a need to serve for universal spiritual satisfaction. Instead, whether they believe or admit it themselves, some start for personal material gratification.

The point I'm trying to make is this: if you're afraid that if you stop tithing to your church that the church is going to shut down, then maybe it might need to if people aren't inspired to give to support it. Or, maybe your church needs to change its spiritual menu?

-$ $ $-

Suppose you're at a restaurant that has a suggestion box. In that case, you can usually fill out a card for compliments or complaints in the hopes that the business will either continue to serve you with excellent service, or give attention to something that could be improved.

Chapter 5

If you love the environment of the restaurant, the people it draws, and the spirit of the owner, then why wouldn't he appreciate you when you say, "I love the food here, sir or ma'am; however, the coffee tastes a little watered down. Would you consider strengthening it for those of us who know and love coffee?"

If he values his customers' opinions, the owner should reply with something like, "You know, I didn't know that. I'll ask my staff about it and see what we can do to change that. How about this? If you experience that again, ask the server if he can put on a fresh pot."

- $ $ $ -

Maybe all your church needs to do is put on a fresh pot of truth. We coffee drinkers know the truth about a fresh pot! A "fresh" pot means something made recently—as in "today," or today's times.

Some pastors have no idea, either by ignorance, or indoctrinated knowledge, that biblical tithing is obsolete. However, MANY know this yet continue to teach it because it could mean losing their property and all of their material pleasures.

If only they had enough faith to believe that like a person who continues to patronize a restaurant after they've been told that they don't have to drink a watered-down message

Tithe from the Hand

anymore, their members may now be inspired to drink two more cups of the truth, or attend two or more services because now the coffee (the Word) compels them to do so.

Chapter 6

How my Mom Thought 'Blessings Could Be Bought'

"Give, and you will receive a gift, and it will return to you in full—pressed down, shaken together to make room for more gifts, running over, and poured into your lap. The amount you give will determine the amount you get back, in the form of healing, a new car, and a husband."
—Malalie 1:5

We often prayed as a family around my mom's bed. Her number one prayer petition was always, "Lord, I thank You

Can't Buy Blessings

for sending my husband home!" From what I remember, my mom and dad separated when I was seven. However, I was around 9 or 10 when she got saved, and they were only married on paper.

This right here shows you where my mom's heart was, and I never once heard her ask for things for herself that the family wouldn't benefit from. Instead, she would always ask that her husband be saved and sent home because what greater blessing could be given to her children and herself than a loving father, a loving husband, and who was a man of God.

Well, guess what? Another revival was coming to town, and our pastor said the guest speaker would bring a Word from God and a promise of miracles! Well, I'll give you one guess of who said she was in and who was bringing her unhappy and reluctant children along, while bumming a ride each and every night with a neighboring gas-money-requesting sister in Christ? You guessed it… my mom!

Now, let's fast forward to my teenage years and begin this new yet familiar journey…

- $ $ $ -

There's nothing more irritating to a pissed-off 15-year-old boy, who would rather be playing his guitar or watching reruns of "Soul Train" or "Good Times", than an angry,

Chapter 6

yelling, fire and brimstone preacher with a speech impediment. Ugh! All I could hear was an emphasis on words that start with "P," the distortion caused by the yelling in the mic, and the feedback sound when he put the mic down after saying, "Praise God?!"

And, of course, to which the audience would answer in the traditional "call and response" ritual "Praise God!" ... but then he said something that caught my attention. The clarity of it surpassed the "p" sounds that his speech impediment had created and was crystal clear.

He said, "God said, if you fast for three days, write three things down on a piece of paper and drop it in this bucket, along with your tithes, God said He was going to give it to you!" Sister Mildred took off running up and down the aisle. Brother Michael played the organ like Stevie Wonder in the zone. Everyone else in the congregation stood up and spoke in so many different tongues that I believe a guest would vow, "Lord, I'll never come back if you get me out alive!"

The drug had taken its effect! He said EXACTLY what poor people needed to put in their eardrums—the hope dope! And it was what my mom needed to hear, as well as myself, because my life changed after that sermon.

The pastor started off with a sneaky, guilt-inducing statement, "I hear from your Pastor that we are having a

Can't Buy Blessings

problem with rodents here... they're called "non-tithers!" We got to get them outta here, Amen?!" The crowd responds, "Amen!"

Then, he went further down that manipulative slope into the depths of every wallet and purse in the room of the gullible, unsuspecting congregation. "How do you expect God to bless you when you're not being obedient to His Word by blessing Him in return?!" Besides a few 'Amens', it got so quiet that you could hear a church mouse tip-toeing! But, of course, that tip-toeing sound was no mouse. Instead, it was the familiar sound of purses randomly clicking open.

Pastor Robbing-some went on to say, "How do you expect these lights to stay on, Amen? How do you expect a pastor to get to church, if he has no car, Amen? How do you expect him to dress in these nice suits, Amen? You want your pastor to look good, don't you... stand up, pastor!" Everyone claps. "Now, how do you expect to get that new building, Amen?!"

That was the last proverbial nail needed to drive into the non-tithing coffin because EVERYBODY wanted that new building! Then, in his next prophe-lying statement, he explained how we all were going to get what we wanted!

Hallelujer, this is what I've been waiting for!

Chapter 6

He said, "God said to write three things you want in any order, fold it up on a piece of paper, bring it up to me and put it in this bucket with your tithes and offerings. If you'll fast for three days, God said He was going to give you each one of those things, Glory!"

The organist was cued to hit that runway chord, and Brother James, who shouted like he was the 6th member of The Jackson 5, took off up the aisle! Whoosh! That brother was sharp dressed, handsome, and had more steps than Nick Caldwell from the legendary R&B group, The Whispers!

This pastor's message also resonated with me so deeply that even I was eager to begin the fast so that everything I wanted would come to fruition—and it did. However, it wasn't because of my sacrifice of three days; it was because of my work for three weeks during the summer break—but more on that later.

- $ $ $ -

My mom decided we were all going on a fast. For the first time in our fasting history, I was more than willing to go without government food, chicken and dumplings, and even my favorite White Castle cheeseburgers, if it was *only for three days*!

Can't Buy Blessings

I could guess what my mother had written down, which was ingrained in my mind from family prayer request time: 1) her husband back home, 2) a car (wait, she ain't got no license), and 3) a new home.

As for me, I wanted a summer job, a new bass guitar, and some new clothes... in that order!

- $ $ $ -

As a teenager, I fell in love with the American band Earth, Wind, and Fire. So when I saw their bassist Verdine White on the inside of the album jacket, I said to myself, "That's what I'm going to do! I'm going to be a bass player." I eventually became one, but more on that later.

Sunday night, I ate my last meal around 11:45 p.m. while everybody else was asleep, so when Monday morning came around, I had a full belly. I was prepared for my blessings to come pressed down, shaken together, and with a new bass guitar poured onto my lap! But guess what? I found out later what that scripture was really about, and that scripture is about "forgiveness," not for "getting."

- $ $ $ -

I have to address something Pastor Robbing-some alluded to earlier: "How do you expect the lights to stay on, if you don't tithe?" The correct answer is through *offerings*. How

Chapter 6

many of my 5% studiers of the Bible (and not just readers) know about the shekel tax? That's right, the shekel tax.

That's how they kept the lights on! **Exodus 30:13** says:

"Each one who crosses over to those already counted is to give a half shekel, according to the sanctuary shekel, which weighs twenty gerahs. This half shekel is an offering to the Lord."

The temple tax was paid by the Israelites and the Levites and went towards the upkeep of the temple—not the tithes because the tithes were food. In other words, pastors' suits, cars, homes, and new buildings, were NOT to be paid for with the biblical tithe; it's to be paid by free will offerings described in the New Covenant!

Y'all go and study **Exodus 30:11-16** for yourselves, and leave me alone, cause I'm getting back to talking about my mom! :-)

Chapter 7

How my Mom Thought 'Wanting' Means 'Getting'

"And my God will meet all your needs out of the material riches of his glory in Christ Jesus." —Malalie 1:6

We get this one wrong all of the time because the scripture doesn't say in **Philippians 4:19**, '*out of* the riches', it says '*according to* His riches.' It's a promise that He will provide your financial, physical, and spiritual needs, not wants.

Chapter 7

What does that look like? It's simple—food, clothes, water, and shelter. That's it... and if you don't have that, it's not because of God's wrath; it's because of man's greed!

But, if you work hard, you can provide your wants, which is what I discovered, and not by fasting, but by using your fundamental abilities and intelligence, unique gifts, and special talents that God already has provided you to use as a tool to manifest all of your wants. Now, back to the fast.

My mom, sister, and two brothers succumbed to the hunger gods and only made it to about 6:30 p.m. that Monday evening; however, I, on the other hand, despite the hunger headaches and growling stomach pains (as if my innards were performing a protest march in my belly), was determined and made it to the second day at noon!

And there wasn't a doubt in my mind that God would hold it against me that I didn't complete the whole three days because there's a scripture that says:

> "23Whatever you do, work at it with all your heart, as working for the Lord, not for human masters, 24since you know that you will receive an inheritance from the Lord as a reward. It is the Lord Christ you are serving."
> —Colossians 3:23-24

Wanting vs Getting

I was indeed rewarded for that action until this present day.

The next day after I ended my fast, I was driven by confidence, positive thinking, and a "knowing," so I applied for a summer job and I got it! "Praise to God! Halapiena! Thank Ya and Glory!"

The job was at the downtown post office delivering mail and it was paying $4 an hour! For a 15-year-old poor kid in the projects, $4 an hour, 40 hours a week, was like making $30 an hour as a UPS driver who's single! Cha-ching!

I was so happy. When I got home and told my mom, she said, "That's great, but how are you going to get there? I don't have any bus fare money." I replied, "That's ok, I'll walk." Thinking to myself, *the devil is a liar!*

She replied, "Alright now! You go ahead and walk then." Teasing her, I "funny-walked" right up those project steps to my room.

To give you an idea of how far that walk was to work, it was a 20-minute drive, which meant I had to get up an hour and a half earlier for two weeks (until I got my first paycheck) to be on time.

I was never late, never called in sick, and never missed a day! Again, I was determined to keep that job for the whole summer, and little did I know, my next two wants were on the way!

Chapter 7

Meanwhile, I realized my mom was looking depressed while still waiting for just one of her wants to sprout just a leaf from the tithes that she had faithfully sown—it was as if she was slowly withering away with every disappointment.

Chapter 8

How my Mom Thought Trusting in a Pastor, Was 'Trusting in God'

"Trust in your pastor with all thine **money**, and suffer financially, unto your own misunderstanding."
—Mala**lie** 1:7

Wrong again. The scripture is "Trust in the Lord with all your heart and lean not on your own understanding," **Proverbs 3:5**. To trust in someone means to believe in, to

Chapter 8

have an absolute dependency on and confidence in someone, and fallible man is not that "One."

Just ask that 92-year-old mother who, after 50 years of membership, wasn't allowed to worship in her church anymore because she stopped tithing!

Ask the single mom who hit the $187 million lottery and was sued by a pastor of a church that she didn't belong to for $10 million dollars!

Ask my mom who, on many occasions, would ask her pastor for help on the rent ($40) only to be told, "Pastor is not in," yet his car is sitting out in front of the church.

It's been said that when you believe in a thing that you don't understand, you suffer... and sometimes, like my mom, they eventually die. Anyway, back to my testimony :)

- $ $ $ -

It's payday! I was excited to receive my first check! I cashed it across the street from work and treated myself to my favorite burgers right next door—White Castles! I finally got to ride the bus home, too, but before I did, I went downtown to the clothes store a few blocks away and put my new clothes on layaway.

And guess what I did next? You guessed it, I went to the music store, picked a bass guitar for $300, and put it on

Trusting in Pastor

layaway! I had done the math and calculated that I would be able to get all of my clothes out before school started, and my bass guitar out on my last check.

I remember saying to myself, "Wow, that pastor was right! I got all three things that I wanted!" However, in reality, all my needs had already been provided by God, as far as food, shelter, and clothing, and my wants are what I had provided for myself through my job.

To wait is to expect, and to act is to receive. To make a long story short, I ended up getting my job, my clothes, and my bass guitar. Even up until you started reading this book, those three wants manifested into more jobs, allowing me to buy more clothes and bass guitars!

That job led to another job at a hotel across the street, where I became a cook for a hotel, those clothes allowed me to draw attention from a crush in high school (I know, I know), and that bass not only led to more bass guitars, it led to playing bass in one of the top bands in my state, which led to moving to California, which led to becoming a world-class musician who's played on numerous recordings, and has toured the world four times over—who stopped tithing over 10 years ago.

Chapter 8

I can honestly say I was blessed more after I stopped tithing and started giving! However, I can also say that a self-analysis led to discovering that by utilizing the gifts I was born with, *waiting* for what I wanted was never going to get me what I wanted unless *acting* followed in pursuit of what I wanted.

I discovered I had an internal intelligence, capable and sound mind, and the logical fortitude needed to solve my financial and physical challenges. My next story may serve as a template for someone.

There is always someone out there with a cure for your ailment, whether mental, emotional, physical, or spiritual. Whether it's credit repair, business investing, weight loss, income tax evasion, or spiritual abuse, somebody has a solution or cure for it—but for a price, and usually with no guarantee for the desperate individual.

This is a con man's paradise because, like a shark that smells blood and then devours its prey, a con man smells your desperation, poverty, and needs and then consumes your money.

They know that the gullible want and need immediate relief, so they provide temporary solutions that sometimes create lifelong and, in some cases, permanent problems. Little do we know that our problems come with a solution attached to them, as I'll demonstrate with my own story of

Trusting in Pastor

how you, too, can find the cause of a problem and administer the right prescription to manage, control, or hopefully solve it.

I wish my mom had been around long enough so that we could come up with solutions that would solve her problems, and we would have started giving more and tithing less.

Chapter 9

How a Mom Can Sometimes Chose 'Me-Search' Over Research

"Those who want to get rich fall into temptation and a trap and into many foolish and harmful desires that plunge people into ruin and destruction." —1 Timothy 6:9

One day, around the age of 16, I started to notice what looked like Chicken Pox around my ankles. They weren't painful; however, they itched for up to 10 days and sometimes would break through the skin. I showed my

Me-Search over Research

mother and she suggested a bath with some alcohol in it... can you say, *OUCH*?!

The alcohol bath was like a thousand bees stinging me at once, but I didn't blame my mother; she was suggesting something that would make me feel better.

My socks and pants would irritate the Chicken Pox-like bumps whenever they rubbed up against them, so I created my own home remedy of putting bandaids with Vaseline on the infected area, because covering them made me feel better.

Years passed, and I eventually visited several doctors who assured me they could find out the problem by addressing the symptoms with numerous lotions, creams, and ointments (which never worked). One doctor even did a biopsy and said, "I couldn't find anything," and he was the top dermatologist in the state!

I prayed for it and even THAT didn't work! Finally, I started to see a pattern where the only thing that these people were able to do was to prescribe or say to me something that made me feel better. Why? Because they had no idea what the cause of this "ankle pox" was!

And then, one day, I had an incredible idea: I'll find out the cause myself.

Chapter 9

- $ $ $ -

I love dogs and I was given a German Shepherd puppy who about three months old. I kept him in the house with me and allowed him to sleep at the foot of the bed, and the next day, I had ankle pox everywhere! I couldn't figure out what happened, so I decided to start by putting the puppy outside for the next day. I woke up, and more ankle pox, along with thigh, arms, and neck pox! I was miserable, and then I noticed a little flea had bitten me!

Then something said to mark an "X" with a permanent marker and check to see what happens. The next day, I woke up, and guess what, there was a blister where the "X" was— I was allergic to fleas! I then noticed that what I thought were specs of dirt were fleas in my bed, in my light-colored clothes, and especially in my socks!

I got flea bombs, steamed the carpet, washed everything in the house, and had to give my beautiful puppy away—but I had discovered my problem and now knew how to manage and control it so I could avoid that level of misery ever again.

- $ $ $ -

How did I discover the cause of my misery? I acknowledged a problem, researched possible causes, gathered the facts, and tested the evidence to find the appropriate solution.

Me-Search over Research

You may have to do this with your church and your personal studies in every area of your life. You have to do the research to find out the cause of the problem and then apply your "me-search."

When you hear these messages every Sunday morning, then Monday through Saturday realize that the problem is still there, it's like being given a prescription for the symptoms that temporarily go away that's only designed to make us feel better. Still, it never addresses the cause of our stress, frustrations, or financial challenges.

We have to do a personal intervention in our lives, shine a light on our problems, research the causes, gather the facts of whether it's controllable, manageable, or curable, then, like a spiritual experiment, test the new information and evidence on ourselves to find out the causes of our own miseries.

Now, let me take a sidebar for just a quick minute before y'all seal up your tithing envelopes for being in fear of the "wrath of Guud" striking you down for using your common sense…

I am not against tithing; I am for "giving." But, I'm not for obligatory tithing as a command, by compulsion, as a fee for church membership, or to remain in good standing so that you can perform with the praise team! Why? Because it's not scriptural and doesn't apply to today!

Chapter 9

We are no longer under the Old Testament law, your pastor is not a Levitical priest, and no one on the praise team, in the church band, or in the congregation is from the tribe of Levi.

You can not put yourself in the place of a Levite, of the tribe of Levi, any more than I can put myself in your family and say I'm your blood!

Chapter 10

How a Mom Can Study To Find Herself 'Confused'

"Study to find thy pastor approved, a member that needed not to be confused, and not questioning how tithing went from being honey, to becoming money." —Mala**lie** 1:9

NOT so fast, Pastor Read-Wrong! The text actually says: "Study to shew thyself approved unto God, a workman that needeth not to be ashamed, rightly dividing the word of truth." —2 Timothy 2:15 (**KJV**).

Chapter 10

If our pastors are not dividing truth, then they are feeding a flock unsound doctrine and a large helping of confusion and misinterpretation. This is important because human beings fundamentally translate and then respond through their interpretation of everything they see, read, and hear based on their cultural, educational, and gender identity knowledge base.

For example, I once witnessed a member greeting my mom after church, and he said to her, "Hello sister, we haven't seen you for a while." She replied, "Oh, I know, I don't have a car and can only catch the bus with my four kids right now." He looks at us, smiles, and then says, "Well sister, we're going to have to get you a car, LOL!"

Now, I knew he didn't really mean he would buy my mom a car; however, because of cultural differences and misinterpretation, my mom heard that he would buy her a car!

Immediately after he said that she started belting out, "Ooh Jesus! He said he was going to get me a car! Glory, thank You, Father! Shum bo- lo- lo- lo!" and so on, but this embarrassed the well-intentioned gentleman and he walked off. We never saw him attend one more service.

From what I remember, my mom was still waiting for that car. People who have never had anything are easily fooled because they've never had anything. If she had asked him, "Do you mean you're going to buy me one?", he could have

A Mom Confused

clarified what he meant, he would still be a member, and she would not be waiting for him to buy that car.

Unfortunately, this kind of misinterpretation continues to be perpetuated in many churches today. This happens because so many believers misinterpret the Bible and confuse the literal with the logical. This next story is a perfect example of when you should apply the logical.

Once, a pastor came into town and said, "If you want to see a miracle, I'm going to show you one on my last night, which will be this Friday, and it will prove to you that there is a living God." Well, who wouldn't want to see a miracle in action, that would end ALL doubts about whether God was real or not, right?! Well, my mom indeed did, and even though I'd prefer to be home doing homework, I was not going to miss that service!

Well, this pastor had that church packed and lined up like they were about to get a free Popeye's fried chicken breast, bacon, and cheese sandwich—everybody wanted one!

Even I, the most skeptical of my family, wanted to witness this so-called miracle because then I would be able to continue believing in the three things my mom always wanted—which were a new home, a new car, and the greatest of the miracles-my father coming home, of which I

Chapter 10

knew would make my mom the happiest. And if anyone deserved to be happy, it was my mom.

"How many of you all are ready to see the power of God in action?" The pastor started his sermon off with this manipulated question. Of course, a vocal flurry of Amen's, hallelujahs, shum bo lo lo's, and glory's responded loudly, like it was the last day of "21 days of prayer, and fasting" — you couldn't wait to get home to eat!

He starts out with a short story about his lifelong dream of wanting to play piano. He asked the audience, "Let's all clap in rhythm, and being at a predominantly black church, we brought the "2 and 4" rhythm... and then I noticed something... he started intentionally clapping off rhythm!

The audience laughed, and then he said, "See, I have not a hint of rhythm, however, how many of us know that our God is a God of miracles, and He will put rhythm where there never was any rhythm, Amen?!"

The church was standing on their feet now! People were jumping up and down in place, crying, speaking in tongues, you name it, the Spirit had entered the room! I was in the church band then, so we had to accent every time he made a praise statement; however, I decided to sit down after what came next.

A Mom Confused

He went over to the piano, sat down, and said, "I've always had a love for classical music, and God said, since you've been obedient and have preached the gospel of my Word, I will bless you with this gift." Then he started to play the most beautiful classically-trained music that anyone in that church had ever heard.

My eyes couldn't help from watering from the embarrassment, and my mouth dropped open, I could not believe that the congregation would fall for this. It was apparent to me that this guy intentionally clapped off rhythm, hadn't played piano all week intentionally, and was about to ask for what? You guessed it... an offering!

When he had finished the familiar piece and the gullible sheep in the audience was done "shouting" in place and in the aisles, he said, "How many of you want a miracle like this in your life?" The response was an overwhelming amount of "Yes Lords!" So he said, "Well then, let's start being obedient in our tithes and offerings!"

There it is—the hook, line, and bank account sinker! If these people hadn't literally accepted that this pastor was actually displaying a miracle and used logic, they would have realized he was playing Beethoven's 5th symphony (with mistakes, mind you). They would have saved themselves some Popeye's chicken sandwich money and left because he had scammed over 90% of the church by falsifying a miracle of God.

Chapter 10

It turned out, after investigation, that he was an undercover classically trained pianist! This, my brothers and sisters, is why we perish because we are blessed at birth with the four things that, if we use them correctly, will help to provide our heart's desire. Those four things are intelligence, common sense, health, and logic. However, like my mom, all those things go out the window when one wants to believe a thing is true.

A miracle is an event that is not explicable by natural or scientific laws, and is therefore considered to be the work of a divine agency. What a miracle isn't is someone who pretends to never have the technical faculty to play classical music, learned how to play it, and now professes that he can now play classical music! That's not a miracle—that's a con.

The only way to determine a miracle is if this person was in a coma, paralyzed in both arms and was playing with their toes! People, the truth will come out as it did on this con artist—no matter how much you or anyone tries to suppress it.

And if it's not revealed outwardly through the love, observation, and intervention shared privately by friends, family, or the eyes of the public, it will take root inwardly and manifest through your awareness and personal responsibilities, and if you're lucky—a call for personal accountability.

A Mom Confused

-$ $ $-

I have other stories, like the pastor who said, "The Lord said to go pick out the car you want" so by faith, you should pick out your car and tell the car dealer the Lord said that you are to give me this car, only to be laughed out of the dealership.

Or the one where the pastor said he drove through a neighborhood he liked and then told the realtor, "God is going to give me that home." She hands over the keys, and if you trusted God, you would do the same, only to be told your credit isn't good enough.

Or the one where the pastor said, "God said to claim it, and it will be yours," and then tells a brother to go and get that car he's trying to buy, to which the brother returns the next day and says, "The interest was higher than I wanted, but I got it!"

When we take things literally, without applying logic, we almost always suffer because we fail to, or don't know how to interpret it correctly, and divide the Word truthfully.

-$ $ $-

If you remember Rod Serling from the Twilight Zone, you can appreciate the humor in my next story: Imagine, if you will, a restaurant that you have been going to out of

Chapter 10

obligation most of your life that serves you nutrient-deficient food at an exorbitant price—your mental, physical, and spiritual well-being. You go there because that's where you have always gone to eat.

Now, imagine that right up the street is another restaurant that allows you to pick your own price yet serves food of the highest nutrient quality and restores your mental, physical, and spiritual well-being. Are you going to continue to go to the restaurant that has nutrient-deficient food out of obligation and at the expense of your soul, or are you going to continue to start to patronize the restaurant right up the street that not only allows you to pay your own price for their food, but you know it's the best quality food that you could give to your body?

The name of today's episode is "All you can eat-for only Free-99"—these questions can only be answered in the "Lie-light Zone!"

The answer should be that you're going to go to the restaurant up the street because if you continue to support the other restaurant with blind loyalty and obligation, it's going to come at a costly expense that is guaranteed to jeopardize your mental, spiritual, and financial health; and if she attends that same restaurant, your mom's as well.

So why would you continue to feed yourself unhealthy food by patronizing a restaurant only because its survival is

A Mom Confused

based on your patronage but is detrimental to the sustenance of your body?

The same is true about your spiritual food. Suppose you continue to go to Reverend Lie-Good's church just because you don't dare to stand up for the truth; in that case, you can expect to live a life in mental, spiritual, and financial misery.

Instead, you should go to Reverend Get-Right's church that allows you to stand on the truth and be served the highest quality mental and spiritual food, where the only expense is your free-will giving, as your heart purposeth.

However, some of you will continue to go to Reverend Lie-Good's church for personal, social, or self-serving reasons that will justify the feeding of faulty spiritual soul food—food that doesn't do anything for your personal well-being, your social circle interaction, or your own spiritual growth.

But those of us who use logic, common sense, and God-given intelligence, we will start to support Reverend Get-Right's ministry without a second thought, without feelings of guilt or responsibility, and without tithing as a command—because we know that the nourishment of our souls takes priority over anyone's feelings, material wealth, or un-sound

Chapter 10

doctrine, in regard to the obsolete tithing laws, that are no longer required of today's believers.

One of the major problems with Christians that don't study to find themselves approved is that they seem to take comfort in just listening, and finding themselves confused.

Chapter 11

How a Mom That's a Tither, Can Really Be a 'Lie-Ther'

"Instead, speaking the truth in love, we will grow to become in every respect the mature body of him who is the head, that is, Christ." —Ephesians 4:15

"Truth" is simply common sense. It's as simple as discovering what happens when you put your hand amid a fire, jump off of your church's balcony, or tithe 10% of what you need for your rent and the landlord gives you an eviction notice. It causes some form of physical, emotional,

Chapter 11

or financial pain, and pain is a warning sign that says you should stop what's causing it.

And, I'm sure by now that most of you "lie-thers"...excuse me...tithers, are screaming at me through the book, "It wasn't tithing that killed your mom!" ... and you'd be right to an extent. The slow poisoning of misinterpretation of what tithing is led to her hardships, poor health, and eventual death. However, I believe it was the pastors in her life that administered it, whether it was unintentional because of their indoctrination, or because of the love of money.

Had she studied the texts clearly and understood them and then applied her God-given common sense, she would have discovered as I have that tithing is not a command, mandate, investment, debt, ransom, bribe, barter, fee, obligation, and not money! It's a tenth. So, if you decide to give a tenth of your income, then by all means, do so.

However, suppose it causes you to feel any guilt for doing so? In that case, you owe it to yourself to search your heart why and then see if it is rooted in indoctrination, ego, or fear—because voluntary tithing and free-will giving should be rooted in love.

Tither vs Lie-Ther

It is my wish that those of you who still have your mom with you, out of love, share this information with her in an effort to help, heal, and honor her in a way that will extend her stay in this world far past the short 57 years that my mom lived.

I've decided to use this chapter as a sort of template, that if you can glean from it anything that will help you bring clarity to one person that's suffering from what I call "tithe-itis"—a condition caused by a breakdown in intelligence, that affects the mind, body, and bank account that is only cured through giving—then my work is complete, my purpose fulfilled, and a mom's life has been changed.

I know my mom will be proud of me and smile from the stars for writing this book. If it helps one person live a guilt-free giving life, then sharing her story affirms that her sacrifice wasn't in vain.

-$ $ $-

The conversation I'm about to have now with my mom—had she lived long enough for me to share this knowledge—is not for my self-aggrandizement. It's to shine a light on an issue that permeates churches today throughout the world through misinterpretation of the truth that continues to persecute the poor, protect the rich, and paralyze personal prosperity by keeping some in the trap of financial bondage.

Chapter 11

This light should also expose pastors who falsely teach and ritually justify, conforming the tithes from produce provided by God back then to profit, which is demanded by man today.

So join me now, if you will, on a journey to my past through love, along with the necessary ingredients of listening, discernment, advice, and release, that I get to have one last conversation to try and relieve, comfort, and save my mom.

Chapter 12

'The Truth in Love' Conversation About Tithing for Moms (and Pastors)

"Dear children, let us not love with words or speech but with actions and in truth." —1 John 3:18

It's a beautiful Sunday morning and my mom is waiting for me to pick her up for church, but this morning will be different. This morning I'm going to get to her house at least an hour earlier because this Sunday, I have a gift to

Chapter 12

share that will require the psychological unwrapping of obsolete and false knowledge to reveal the natural and real truth of tithing.

I get to my mom's home, knock on the door, and greet my mom with a hug. She greets me with the usual, "Hello handsome, I'm still getting ready." (All of us know when we go to pick Mom up, she's always 'still' getting ready). "Go get you some potatoes out the skillet if you want some."

"Yum!" I replied, "I think I do want some!"

Then I grabbed a plate, lifted the glass lid off the skillet on her old stove, and the wonderful smell of fried potatoes and onions filled my sinuses… and shortly, it will be filling my belly!

While I'm eating, she sits down at the table to put on her shoes, and while putting one foot in, she says, "What's so important that you want to discuss before church? You know pastor don't like people walking in late. Oh, and loan me $20, you know I can't go to church empty handed."

My mother would often borrow money from me, Mr. Jacobs, or sometimes even the church member sitting next to her— only to put it into the offering plate. She would justify borrowing what she didn't have by saying things like, "Shoot! I ain't trying to miss my blessing… you know it's better to give than receive. LOL!" she'd declare.

Truth in Love

- $ $ $ -

I finish off my potatoes, wipe my face with the paper napkin, and have a sip of Kool-Aid. "Ok, I'll give you this $20," I replied, "But only if we can have a quick Bible study. I have good news to share in regard to giving versus tithing."

Mom, preoccupied with getting ready for church, replies, "Ok, but I don't want to be late. Here, take one of these Snickers bars." She gets on both shoes, then says, "Now, what about this giving versus tithing?"

I clear my throat nervously, then I softly say, "Well, Mom, I've watched you give 10% or more of every increase you receive as I've grown up, and that belief was indoctrinated and adopted by me as well, until just a few weeks ago… and I won't be tithing anymore."

Mom's eyes got big, looked at me like I used the Lord's name in vain, then said, "Boy, what do you mean? You ain't tithing anymore?"

Glancing around the room for what could possibly be thrown at me, I reply, "Nope, not another cent, Mom. New Covenant giving is all that's required today, mom, and that's giving as your heart purposeth, and not as Passa demandeth!"

Chapter 12

My mom's body language suddenly shifts, and her fists subconsciously ball up. Watching her carefully, though, I went on.

"See, Mom," I added, "We've been taught that we have to give 10% of our income in order to be blessed, and if we don't, we'll be cursed. However that's not true, and it never was for us."

Mom now has a little sweat forming on her forehead, stands up, then says, "The blood of Jesus! Lord, please don't strike him down in my kitchen before I give his $20 to you! God of Abraham, Isaac, and Jerome! Have you lost your mind, boy?"

Noticing she has just picked the fly swatter up off the wall- and there's no fly to be seen, I lower the volume of my voice and say, "No Mom, quite the contrary, in fact, I've found it."

Now the fly swatter is being swung in circles like she's next up at bat with bases loaded and about to hit a grand slam with my head as the ball!

I continued, "And I've used my mind to do the research, studied to find myself approved, and have been transformed by renewing my mind and my bank account!"

Now, she's subconsciously hitting the side of the table, and I can see her bottom lip folded up. Usually, what that meant growing up was the closest person to her was about to get swatted, so I slowly scooted back in my chair out of fly swatter reach.

I swallowed hard, and then I said, "Christians, or someone not of Jewish descent, weren't required to tithe either, Mom, or have an obligation to tithe today. Only the children of Israel in the promised land of that time were required to obey this law, which was one of the 613 commandments. And guess what else I found out?"

Now, both her eyebrows are raised, and I'm starting to question if I should continue to put my life at risk or not...

Then she says, "Oh Lord, let me sit down, and get my Bible ready, 'cause I know I'm about to do some swatting, and some rebuking up in here!" So she sits down, makes a "whew" sound, and then says, "Now, what else did you find out, boy, before I have to get out my anointing oil?"

Feeling just a little safer now, I say to her, "Ok, I'm glad you are sitting down for this... I found out that it was never money, it was food! The tithes were to be eaten, not spent!"

Mom looked at me and gasped like I cussed out her pastor. Then she loudly says, "Lord ham mercy, with biscuits and gravy! Where in the world did you hear that, boy?!"

Feeling that now that I no longer have to wonder if the screen door is locked, I reply, "Well, Mom, the Old Testament makes it clear, however, we've been ignorant to

Chapter 12

the clarity of the scriptures because we've always read on past this truth, instead of noticing it to stop and study it."

She fidgets in her chair a little bit. I continue, "We relied on our pastor's translation and interpretation of them instead of studying them for ourselves, Mom, and applying their understanding of the texts to our personal lives. You see, Mom, most of us just read our Bibles; however, very few of us study our Bibles, statistically, and that's where we do ourselves a disservice."

Suddenly becoming interested in that unknown fact, she screams out, "Father in Heaven on a holy roller coaster! Where's that never money part at, boy, LOL?!"

Now that she's laughing a little, I'm feeling a little less threatened, and I respond with, "Yes ma'am and we've been on that holy roller coaster a little too long, Mom, time to jump off, and open up your Bibles!"

- $ $ $ -

She grabs her Bible from the end of the table, implying that she's ready. Then I say, "If you turn to Leviticus 27:30, it says, A tithe of everything from the land, whether grain from the soil or fruit from the trees, belongs to the LORD; it is holy to the LORD."

Truth in Love

Then I point outside the window and say, "Do you own any land, Mom? Do you have a field? Do you see money in that scripture, Mom?"

Then she leans back in her chair and says, "JESUS!!! And that's why we, and our money, my money, perish!" Then she bursts into song, singing, "Jesus on the mainline, tell Him what you want, well, I want my money back! LOL!"

My mother listened to gospel music all day, so I knew more songs would come in response to our conversation!

"Exactly my thoughts too, Mom!" In an effort to comfort her, I reply, "But Mom, there's nothing wrong with giving a tithe, only paying a tithe as the children of Israel did because the work on the cross ended that, according to Scripture."

Mom replies, "Boy, you better preach on this fine Sunday, that the Lordeth hath made!"

I smile subtly and share more with her. "In John 19:30, when Jesus said, 'It is finished,' there was no more need for sacrifices or levitical temples, or the tithing law…! And guess what else…?"

Mom feels a little overwhelmed with this new Scriptural interpretation, leans back in her chair, and says, "Wait, boy, let me take a swig of my Pepsi first!"

Chapter 12

She takes a big swig and puts the bottle down as if to say she's ready. "Ok, I'm ready, Jesus in a manger, in an Air BnB!" I burst out in laughter, mainly because that visual is hilarious.

"Ok..go ahead, boy," she says, anxiously awaiting more of this good news.

"Ok, and get this, Mom... the tithes weren't even to be paid to the pastor, the tithes were to be paid to the Levites of the tribe of Levi for their work in the temple!"

Mom pushes her Bible away and yells, "The Levites?! What the heck is a Levite, boy?"

I slowly push her Bible back to her and say, "If you go to Numbers 18:21, it says, 'I give the Levites all the tithes in Israel as their inheritance in return for the work they do while serving at the tent of meeting.' Does our pastor come from the tribe of Levi?"

Mom leans toward me and says, "Humph, after hearing this and visualizing his big potbelly, he might be from the tribe of Rib-eye, but I don't know about no Levi! LOL!"

I almost spit out my Kool-Aid into the Scripture jar to keep it from coming through my nose, trying to control my laughter! "Ok boy don't be messing up my table cloth!" she says jokingly. Then she says, "That's OK because I'm giving my tithes to Jesus, anyway and…"

Truth in Love

"El contraire mon frère!" I interject. "No, no, and NO! That's not OK either, Mom under the tithing law, because Jesus wasn't a Levite."

"Hush boy!" she blurts out as if I dared try to take Jesus' money.

"His father was Joseph of the tribe of Judah," I reply, "And he was not of the Levitical priesthood, in fact, that would have been a sin because it would be a transgression of the Jewish law."

Mom's heart, mind, and mouth are wide open now—and she might even be in shock, but I go on.

"In other words, you tithing to Jesus is like you paying back my $20 to the church instead of me. I'm the one you owe it to, not the church!"

"Wait, fool, and when did you learn French?!" she says jokingly in an attempt to divert from the discussion.

- $ $ $ -

Then while using her heels to take off her shoes, she grabs last Sunday's church fan and says, "Boy, I will smack you with this church fan if you're lying on my Jesus!"

"No weapon formed shall posture, Mom!" I pronounce.

Chapter 12

"That's PROSPER, devil, not posture," she replies, and we laugh.

Then she says inquisitively, "So, tithing to Jesus would have been a sin?!"

"Yes Ma'am," I emphasizes, "and you giving my $20 back to anyone else but me would be a sin against me, too!"

She grabs the fly swatter, and I say, "Just kidding!"

She smiles, and I cautiously continue with, "So, actually, Mom, churches that are requiring tithes under the law today are really sinning, because they're collecting and gathering money for the storehouse, instead of collecting and gathering produce for the storehouse, which God commanded to go to the Levites."

Mom raises up in her chair and says, "So the pastor is receiving tithes that don't belong to him?"

I reply, "Yes, that would be correct, Mom, if he's teaching from the Old Covenant law. Jesus would have never taken a tithe, Mom, because He knew it belonged to the Levites, therefore He would have tithed to the Levites, not Himself."

"Um, um, um!" she grunted in an effort to process this new knowledge.

Truth in Love

Then I go on with, "Did you know, there was actually a storehouse, too?"

Mom takes off her wig and lays it on the table as if to say, "That's it!" So now one of two things are about to happen: either somebody's about to get a whoopin', or we about to have church up in here!

Mom takes a swig of Pepsi, then says, "God of Abraham, Isaac, and Jerome, don't you get us struck down in here, boy, especially before I get to eat my Kentucky Fried Chicken!"

Then I said, "Wait, what…when was Kentucky Fried Chicken discussed?" She winks as if to say, "The Kentucky Fried Chicken you're about to be buying!"

I chuckle a little and then reply with, "That's God of Abraham, Isaac, and Jacob, Mom… not Jerome."

She goes from a smile to a straight face in two-seconds flat, and then I respectfully continue.

"But anyway," (clearing my throat) "Yep, there was actually a storehouse, and neither you, me, or pastor, or any Christian, would have been allowed to enter it without getting arrested, imprisoned, or if the guard was Phinehas, son of Eleazar, we could even get get impaled!"

Chapter 12

She grabs her Bible, licks a fingertip, and says, "And where is this, Pastor Mokolo?"

I mock our pastor's voice and say, "Nehemiah 10:38 says, 'And the priest the son of Aaron shall be with the Levites, when the Levites take tithes: and the Levites shall bring up the tithe of the tithes unto the house of our God, to the chambers, into the treasure house.'"

I let her read and marinate on that for a minute or two, and then I go on, "In other words, you can bring your money to the bank, but you better not try to take your money behind the counter!"

She interrupts and says, "Not unless you want a bullet in your butt, LOL!"

I smile and say, "Yes ma'am!" then I continue with, "The levitical temple was for worship, Mom, not for storing money or produce."

Mom closes her Bible as if to have an "aha" moment and says, "Boy, you mean to tell me, that the church ain't the storehouse?"

I shake my head and say, "Nope, not back then, and definitely not today, except for when of course a pastor teaches that it is, which would be a lie."

Truth in Love

Mom looks at me as if she's starting to get a little angry and says, "I thought the storehouse was the church all this time?!" She looks away in thought, then looks back at me and says, "So, while they are gathering money in their storehouse, I've just been gathering bills in my house?!"

"Yes Ma'am!" I reply.

She slaps her hands on her knees, then says, "Father, give me scrength, because my flesh is getting weak and I'm about to cuss out a passa, LOL!"

Enjoying this conversation's sense of humor, I spoon-fed a little more tasty scriptural hors d'oeuvres with her.

"I used to believe that too, Mom, until I read that there actually was a storehouse. If you turn to Malachi 3:10, it says it clearly, 'Bring the whole tithe into the storehouse, that there may be food (meat) in my house. Test me in this, says the LORD Almighty, and see if I will not throw open the floodgates of heaven and pour out so much blessing that there will not be room enough to store it.'"

Mom blurts out, "Yes Lawd, I know that Scripture!"

Then I say, "But isn't it interesting that 3:11 is left out, which says, 'I will rebuke the devourer for you, so that it will not destroy the fruits of your soil—meaning food from the land—and your vine in the field shall not fail to bear, says the LORD of hosts.' Which, in proper context, is

Chapter 12

talking about their promised land, and not today's church—or you. However, those floodgates need to be opened for those blessings to grow and flow!"

Mom shakes her head, raises her hands, and says, "Yes Lawd, halapiena, thank ya! Open up the floodgates!"

I hated to have to steal her joy like a hungry man with a declined debit card at Chic-fil-et after a three-hour church service; however, I had to interject.

"Slow your holy roll, Mom, those floodgates were rain, which comes from the sky, the heavens, and 'room enough to store' means what grows as a result of the rain goes into the storehouse! The blessings they received weren't material things, Mom, they were agricultural produce."

Mom's blessing smile is now upside down, so she yells, "Jesus of Lazarus!"

I almost said, "No, that's Jesus of Nazareth, Mom," in fun; however, sensing I needed to leave well enough alone, I chose to continue.

- $ $ $ -

"It was also to store produce of grain, wine and oil, all kinds of cattle and sheepfolds," I add, "which is found in other Scriptures in the Bible. In other words, Mom, that would be like going to your bank, and you seeing your money next to

Truth in Love

some vegetables and cattle... you ain't going to ever see that!"

Mom puts up her coat, sits back down, and then says, "Let me get comfortable, boy. I ain't going nowhere now, because I feel like we are having church right here today!"

(See, I told you, either somebody's getting whoopin' or we having church!)

Then she puts on her comfy house shoes and takes a big bite of her Snickers bar, followed by another swig of Pepsi. Then she says, "Ok, Rev, so, how did the churches back then keep the church lights on, and how did they pay into the building fund, and pay the church staff? Shoot!...Sister Odell said she quit playing piano because the pastor wasn't paying her anything but "free99," LOL!"

I said to myself, "And If you ever heard Sister Odell play, you'd know that free99 was too much!"

"Well, technically Mom," I reply, "they were never paid because the tithes were never money, but there was a shekel tax we'll discuss later. Pastors today perpetuate this false doctrine by changing what used to be a commandment between God and the children of Israel, into a tradition between them and the members of the church!"

The shock of this new information is slowly sinking in with Mom, and she astonishingly says, "It really was never

Chapter 12

money?! Precious Lord, take my hand before I slap somebody!"

Then amid our laughter she asks, "Where's that at, boy?! Wait,.. let me put this church fan down and turn the floor fan on and take another swig, because I'm having hot flashes thinking about that 'never money' part, and matter of fact... why don't you just sum all this up in a sermon?!"

She takes a big swig, sits the bottle down and says, "Ok Passa, bring it!"

I'm feeling the Reverend Get-Right spirit about now, so I am preparing to answer her and also have some fun with my impersonation of our pastor—this will be a lot of fun!

- $ $ $ -

Now, if you've been raised in a baptist or holiness church growing up, you can envision and thoroughly enjoy this next part.

If you had a pastor who sang the sermon, then said "Hah!" after each sentence. Just insert the accompanying organ sound after the "Hah!" for the full church experience—and you can interactively add your own "Jesus's, My God's, Preach, Say it again, Watch your mouth now, and Hallelujers" in between the Hah's if you feel led to.

Truth in Love

Get ready now to be a part of Reverend Get-Right's congregation!

- $ $ $ -

I stand up, poke out my belly, walk around the table, and say in the pastor's loud and expressive voice, "Ok chuch, remember, hah, we established that there was the tithe of the land, hah, and the tithe of the flock, right? Hah!

She replies, "Yes, hah!"

I continue, "Well, hah, the only time money was allowed as the tithe, hah, was in Leviticus 27:31 where it says, hah, And if a man will look at all redeem, hah, that's, buy back, hah, ought of his tithes, hah, he shall add thereto the fifth part thereof, hah!" (Add big organ swell here)

Mom yells out an enthusiastic, "Gawd almighty!"

I continue with my sermon and grab her empty Pepsi bottle to use as my microphone.

"Mother! Hah, I said, Mother! Hah, mooooooootherrrraaa! Hah, do you own a field of vegetables?" Hah!

"No suh!"

"Or grains we don't know about?" Hah!

"No suh!"

Chapter 12

"Well then, tithing, hah, has nothing to do with you! Hah, and if you had cattle, hah, there was no redemption, hah, no redemption, hah, I said no redemption, hah, permitted for that at all!"

Mom yells out, "Boom shaka- laka- laka! Jesus!"

(Did she just say?..)

Trying not to be distracted by the obvious song lyrics disguised as speaking in tongues, I continue bringing the *Word of Gawd*.

"So, in other words, hah, if you wanted to buy back some greens and fried chicken, hah, that was the Lawd's, hah, you had wanted back for Sunday dinner, hah, it was going to cost you a little bit more, hah, to buy back God's greens, hah, but you couldn't buy back God's fried chicken!"

Mom yells out, "Hallelujer! That's God's Kentucky fried chicken!"

Then I scream into the Pepsi bottle, "Somebody say Glory to God!" Then we pretend the music kicks in, she stands up, and we both start shouting in place!

Mom laughed and then said, "Now you are making me hungry! And, you know what? I'm going to take this $20 and tithe it to Colonel Sanders and get a bucket of KFC for dinner... now that I know I don't have to pay my tithes, Hallelujer!"

I shake my head and knowing I had just got played for $20, I ask, "Could I at least get the big piece of chicken?"

She ignores my request and asks, "Ok, so how did they pay for these Levitical Temples to run, again...and you know, pay for gas, lights, water bill...ahem, and that building fund?"

I sit down, grab my highlight-filled Bible, take a swig of Kool-Aid and say, "Ahhh, well, I'm glad you finally asked Mom because the building fund back then was called *The Shekel Tax*."

Mom holds her Bible up like she's about to swat me for laughing during testimony service when brother James was obviously drunk.

Then she says, "What?! Boy, don't you be lying in my house now on no Sunday! The shekel what?"

I lower my arms from protecting my head and say, "I'm not lying Mom, It was an annual tax that was the equivalent of about two days work, which was used for the upkeep of the temple. Most Christians don't even know this because we seldom study our Bibles, and it's never taught by pastors because it might mess with their Escalade money! LOL!"

Chapter 12

Mom snaps back, "Well, they are about to miss out on Escalade, lemonade, and Medicaid money, if what you are saying is true!" she says jokingly. "Pass me your Snickers bar..."

I say to myself, "What the...? I was about to open that Snickers bar and was already tasting it..."

"Well, anyway," raising my voice a little, unhappy and Snicker-less.

Then, with a little attitude, as I push my Snickers bar towards her saying, "Exodus 30: 11-16 explains that the shekel tax was the primary source of income for the upkeep of the temple, and to pay for expenses."

"Is that right?" she says, teasingly taking a big bite of my Snickers bar.

"If you can add up to two days' pay," I say, as I watch her enjoying MY Snickers bar, "times a little over three million Jewish males, you'll see there was plenty of money for the building fund. Today's tithes are posing as a sort of shekel tax, that's really the pastor's, and the staff's salary, along with the church's mortgage payment."

"Wait, don't that mean the majority of the tithes go to them?" Mom asks.

Truth in Love

"Yes Ma'am," I reply. "You see, back then the tithes included, and benefited everyone from the stranger to the widow, whereas todays' tithes benefit mainly the pastors' business, disguised as benefitting the members."

Appearing a little overwhelmed and deep in thought, she stared out the window, then replies, "Wait boy,..ooh Jesus..what about robbing God, the curse for not tithing, and all those blessings that were to come from tithing?"

I watch her eat the last bite of my Snickers bar and say, "Yeah Mom, the idea of trying to rob God is as scary as getting caught trying to find loose change in your Moma's purse—the consequences could be fatal! LOL! However, in Malachi 3:8, where it says, Will a man rob God? Yet ye have robbed me. But ye say, Wherein have we robbed thee? In tithes and offerings—Malachi is not talking to us, he's fussing at the people of Judah who lived in Palestine at that time, not the citizens of America of *our* time. Ministers use this scripture out of context like a guilt prod to prod money out of purses and our wallets!"

"So, we're not cursed if we don't tithe?" she asks.

"That would be a curse-free no, Mom," I reply. "Those people were cursed with a curse, Mom, because they weren't tithing their best produce, or tithing blemished animals, or sometimes not at all!"

Chapter 12

"My Gawd!" she yells out.

"What that looks like Mom, is I've got 10 bushels of good greens for me, but if I don't tithe that tenth bushel of greens today, I can have enough for the family reunion next week! So I justify keeping those good greens for selfish reasons, thereby disobeying the law and dishonoring the covenant."

"Heaven help them!" she pleads as if to shutter at the very thought of stealing what belongs to God.

I go on explaining the example and say, "Plus, I can probably give God that calf with only one good ear, instead of one of my good ones with two good ears. He won't mind, He created them, too." LOL!

Mom yells out, "Wait! My Sweet Lord, and a hot peach cobbler! How are you going to think you can keep God's greens, because you want them for the family reunion?! Heck, you wouldn't have any greens if God didn't grow them!"

Then her imagination got the best of her, and she says, "And, who wants a one-ear calf? You have to stand on the one ear side, every time you want it to do something! Humph, that's like making a chicken dinner for God and you give God the little piece of chicken... my God gets the big piece of chicken!" she jokes.

Truth in Love

- $ $ $ -

Then we both hear her stomach growl like a bear awakened from three months of hibernation.

"Ooh, I'm hungry now, call KFC for that 15-piece family meal and a liter of Big Red for pick up."

I say to myself, "Uhh, and who's paying for that?!"

While looking in my wallet to make sure I have enough and chuckling, I continue, "Ok, Mom, last but not least, the blessings we seem to take for granted are our sound mind, our health, and our inherent gifts, and it's through these three things utilized by the God in us that with perseverance, due diligence, and commitment, we can have our materialistic *Heaven on Earth*."

Mom laughs and throws the $20 bill I gave her at me, then says, "Somebody pass the offering plate, cause somebody is getting a love offering today!"

I pick up the money that she is really giving to me to go towards that KFC dinner, then I say, "Philippians 4:13 says it another way, Mom, which is I can do all things through Christ who strengthens me, however, that doesn't mean through playing the lottery, through checks in the mail, or through tithing. It means by taking action through the God within you."

Chapter 12

"Amen, Pastor Eat-Right!" she agrees while hinting she was hungry.

"How are we going to get our KFC 15-piece meal if we just wait on it, right? We've got to go get it, right?" I strongly emphasize.

Mom throws a napkin at me and says, "Boy, you better pass the offering plate one more gain 'cause you are preaching today! But I know you better end this service soon before my stomach growls again!"

Then she ponders for a second and says, "But what would happen if everybody stopped tithing? Wouldn't the churches close down? Shoot, I like to watch, er uh, I mean praise, while Brother's James is shouting!" she stutters shyly.

I say to myself, "Um hum, I knew she liked Brother James..."

Then I respond, "That's simple, a church Gofundme account! Just kidding! However, it's about the same idea because those who can give more would cover for the ones who can't give more, in order to reach a goal. If everyone stopped tithing out of obligation, then they'd have to start giving out of inspiration, and that would show the true heart of that church and a reflection of that ministry."

Truth in Love

Then the church would have to depend on a percentage of faith offerings instead of a percentage of your gross income, which means giving would be by inspiration, as opposed to obligation. Any church will survive, whether teaching sound doctrine or not, as long as its congregants support it.

From the corner of my eye, I see Mom slowly taking back the $20 she threw back at me, then she says, "Wait, Reverend Get-Right, but I thought tithing was giving a tithe to God? Isn't tithing a gift to God?"

I pretend not to see that she slipped that $20 back under the table mat and reply, "First and foremost, I don't believe God would accept the tithes because what would be the point of Jesus's death? That would be like you paying for the KFC dinner after I had already paid for it!"

"Heck, I ain't paying for it at all, but I see what you mean!" Mom confesses.

I say to myself, "Not with your money, you ain't paying for anybody's KFC!" I chuckle and then go on.

"However, I believe a personal, voluntary tithe as a gift would be acceptable, Mom. Because tithing and giving are two different things. One is an obligatory tenth of your income, called tithing, and the other is a voluntary free-will offering or gift from your income, rightly defined as giving. However, some of today's pastors abuse, misuse, and

Chapter 12

misapply the levitical tithing law by calling it a command or *gift* in today's church to manipulate the congregants into giving more than they can."

"Ain't that the truth, pastor! Last week I had to decide between giving a tithe, and getting a bottle of Hennessy."

"MOM!" I yell out, "I didn't know you drank?!"

She smiles slyly and says, "Didn't Jesus turn water into Henny?"

"No, that was wine, not Hennessy!" I cry out.

She laughs and says, "I'm just being silly, Pastor Mokolo, ha-ha! Preach on, Rev!"

I muster up a little fake laugh, along with a side eye, however, I still wasn't convinced she was only being silly.

"Those pastors who teach this today," I go on, "should either repent and start teaching the truth or close their church down, and as Grandma would say, *Take several seats and sit down somewhere* until they are ready to rightly divide and share the truth! Tithing was never a gift, Mom, it was a tax!"

Almost choking on her Pepsi, she puts the bottle down quickly and says, "A TAX?! Like the IRS type tax?"

Truth in Love

"Yes, Ma'am," I reply, "very similar. It was part of a taxation system that maintained the temple; in fact, there were three different tithes. They were:

The Levitical tithe happened in a seven-year cycle and was solely for the Levites.

The Festival tithe, which happened every 1st, 2nd, 4th, and 6th year, within the seven-year cycle, that everyone could partake in, and then;

The Poor tithe happened in the 3rd and 6th year and was for everyone and anyone in need. I don't know about you, but I count seven times within seven years that the tithe was collected. Meanwhile, pastor is collecting every Sunday! But, anyway…"

There was a **fourth tithe** if you want to include the **tithe of the tithe**, which the Levites tithed to the priests from their tithe. However, the food was consumed by the poor and hungry and used for provision. Still, the only profit came from selling to a stranger or alien to the country."

- $ $ $ -

Mom rocks back and forth slowly in her chair, then mumbles, "Lord, I know the song says, Let us break bread together, but the pastor needs to change his menu quick…

Chapter 12

because right about now, I'm about to shut him down with an "F" rating for False Teaching!"

I chuckle a little, and then I ask her, "What would happen if a restaurant that served low quality food shut down? Wouldn't that be better for the community's physical health? Would you continue to support it? Customers would now have to start going to the restaurants who provide better quality food, right?"

Mom responds, "You know that's right, and I'm gettin real hungry now with all this food talk."

Knowing that means it's time to go get the KFC, I continue on while putting on my coat and say, "The same would be true if a church shuts down, that serves the low-quality food of false doctrine, people would now start going to churches that are better for their spiritual health and get this mom?"

"What pastor?" she asks as she points to her stomach.

I lean towards her, like I'm about to gossip about Sister Shirley's raisin potato salad and whisper softly, "The truth doesn't care about how many members a church has, only a pastor not speaking the truth does!"

Mom points her finger up like a woman about to go to the bathroom during the offering, and says, "Aaaaamen! Speak the truth and maim the devil, Hallelujer!"

Truth in Love

I wait a few seconds for her to calm down and say, "Mom, that's a shame the devil, not maim the devil."

She points at me and says, "Shame, maim... it's the same thing! Now, wait, now I know I read somewhere about the tithes being paid in the Old Testament before the law? If that's true, then hasn't there always been a law to tithe? Ummm, hmm..."

"Uh, "BZZZZZT!" (that's the buzzer sound of a wrong answer on a tv game show) I continue, "that would once again be an emphatic NOPE! If you mean Abraham and Jacob's tithe they were both voluntary, and not from a mandate. Abraham tithed from the spoils of war which isn't income, and Jacob's tithe was more of 'If you do this/I'll do that' type of thing—more like a business deal. That custom was most likely adopted from the pre-mosaic tithing custom that was practiced by the pagans, Romans, Chinese, Babylonians, and other cultures of the East."

"Did you just use the P word?" Mom shouts! "Boy, did you say pagan?! Let me get my anointing oil because you might be about to split hell wide open with that foolishness! But, seriously, boy, we were all told that you're not really saved if you don't tithe, and that you're not covered, either. Is that a lie, too? Because I don't want no curses given and no blessings blocked!"

Chapter 12

While walking towards the front door, I smile and say, "Yes, and No, Mom, it was a pagan practice and it was used in other cultures to show appreciation through sacrifices and gifts. But it was never a Divine law until the covenant was established. In our culture today, tithing is no longer a requirement to get into Heaven or to be saved because the gift of salvation is free according to Ephesians 2:8, which says, For by grace you have been saved through faith; and that not of yourselves, it is the gift of God."

I continue, "And in regard to tithing to keep from being cursed and not receiving blessings, the curse was nailed to the cross with Him as said in Colossians 2:14, which says, He canceled the record of the charges against us and took it away by nailing it to the cross."

Mom gets up and moves the table over, and I ask, "What are you doing?"

She pushes the table against the wall and says, "I'm just making some room because I'm about to shout up in here!" Then she puts her hand on the edge of the table, and we mock and shout in place!

"We are having chuch up in here today," she announces in the doorway, and we laugh together as I help her get her coat on.

Truth in Love

Then I say as while opening the door, "Remember, Romans 8:1 says, Therefore there is now no condemnation at all for those who are in Christ Jesus."

Mom belts out an "Amen!" then she starts singing with an invisible tambourine, "There is powder, powder, wonder-working powder, in the blood of the Lamb, Amen!"

I pretend there's a TV camera, look directly into the lens and the audience, and say, "Um, um, um, just lift her up in prayer, y'all!" then I shake my head.

Mom adjusts my coat collar, then says, "So Jesus... really did pay it all?"

I reply confidently, "I'd bet you your big piece of chicken on that, Mom! Oh, and it's wonder working power, not wonder-working powder, so..."

Mom grabs my coat jacket, tugs it, and says, "Boy, you know what I mean...correct me one more time, you hear, and you just might be going up to yonder to be with your Lord soon and very soon!"

"Uh, yes ma'am," I obediently reply as I close her front door on our way out.

Chapter 12

We get into the car, and I continue from where I left off. "But anyway, Mom, remember what Paul said in 2 Corinthians 9:7 that Each one must give as he has decided in his heart, not reluctantly or under compulsion, for God loves a cheerful giver? The emphasis is on a *cheerful* giver, not a *fearful* giver. Unfortunately, today's pastors have twisted the scriptures and made a noose of guilt, shame, and fear to fit over the necks of gullible but sincere and honest believers."

Mom, I notice, is now starting to tear up a little as we pull off. She says, "You know, son, this is all good news and all, however, for almost 20 years I've been a faithful tither, and most times, I gave more than I had because the guest speakers, the prophets, and my pastors said God commanded it, and that I would be blessed with the desires of my heart. Yet instead of getting the desires, I've just gotten the broke-ness of my heart." Her voice fades. Her eyes drop to the floor.

"I know, Mom," I reply sympathetically, "I am a living witness to your seemingly limitless amount of faith, however, we can look at this as a blessing in disguise because we have exposed the wolves in sheep's clothing, that's been poisoning the sheep with false doctrine. The water of truth today has removed that toxin from you today, tomorrow, and forever!"

"Amen, son…Amen," she sadly replies.

Truth in Love

We pull into the Kentucky Fried Chicken parking lot, and the fragrance of fresh fried chicken seem to help shift her mood. Unfortunately, the food is not ready yet, so I share more scripture with her.

"If this is any consolation for you, Mom, 1 Timothy 6:3, 4 says that If anyone teaches a different doctrine and disagrees with the sound words of our Lord Jesus Christ and the teaching that accords with godliness, he is puffed up with conceit and understands nothing. He has an unhealthy craving for controversy, and for quarrels about words, which produce envy, dissension, slander, evil suspicions."

Seeing I have her full attention, I continue, "And if we continue to read verses 5 through 19 of that same chapter, we will have the confirmation we need to know, that the tithing law under the law applied to today is false doctrine."

"Humph," Mom grunts, "may Jesus have mercy on their souls because I'm not going to come to Wednesday Night Bible study!" She continues, "Now, why would they lie on the Word of Gawd?" she says in a jokingly manner but with serious intent. "They know the Word says It's better to throw a birthstone around your neck than to cause one of my little ones to stumble—praise the Lawd!"

"Moma," I say, trying to hold back screaming in laughter, "That's a millstone, not a birthstone!"

Chapter 12

"Jesus make you a vessel, boy! I knew that millstone didn't sound right!" she cackles, "you know that makes so much sense now because I was wondering where are you going to find a birthstone that big?"

While I'm still laughing about the birthstone, she continues on, "Anyway, go ahead now with what you were explaining…and stop laughing at your moma! Now, why do they keep preaching this nonsense if they know it's not the truth?"

Chuckling and wiping away tears of laughter, I reply, "Mom, they do it because they can. No one in today's churches is holding their pastors accountable for perpetuating false teaching for real profit, prioritizing financial gain over spiritual gain, and loving money more than they love Christ. With this truthful revelation of the scriptures, we and others who have transitioned from *believing to knowing* can now use it to free ourselves from the lies about tithing and discover the truth about giving."

Suddenly, my mother stops walking and with seriousness in her tone says, "Now I believe that this explains why nothing I prayed for, not one thing, or any of my desires for my family and me ever came into fruition. Instead, I was blindly tithing money, which I should have seen was really part of my provision that the scriptures speak of."

Truth in Love

She went on with her new revelation, "In Matthew 6: 26,27 it says to look at the birds of the air; they do not sow or reap or store away in barns, and yet your heavenly Father feeds them. Are you not much more valuable than they? Can any one of you, by worrying, add a single hour to your life?"

Then her mood changes as she realizes her release, and she shares, "I could have used that money to provide you all with more food, more clothing for school and church, and maybe even a better home. I also could have provided that much-needed medicine for myself so that I could be in better health to get a better job! Heck...even Jesus was a carpenter when He wasn't teaching! LOL!"

I try to comfort and console her by saying, "Yes, but that was then, the past Mom, and this is the now... and NOW you can stop giving and you can start getting!"

Mom bursts into song, "Amazing Grace, how sweet the sound of that! Stop giving, and start getting!" She says as we walk toward the entrance to KFC.

I open the door for her and say, "Yes ma'am, and what I mean is to stop giving the Biblical tithe that these False Profits are teaching from the Old Testament, and start giving a free-will offering from your heart as the New Testament suggests. And also, start getting the things you need TODAY to maintain your fundamental needs of food, shelter, and clothing! But on another note, Mom, let's get

Chapter 12

this KFC because my stomach is growling and interrupting this service, like that loud co-pastoring Sister Gail in morning service!"

"Yeah," Mom responds, "she calls herself anointed when she's really just a-nnoying, LOL!"

We get the chicken, and Mom adds four cinnamon biscuits to the order without asking me. I say to myself, "No you didn't!"

As we walk to the car, she asks, "You mean I should pay my rent, buy my family's clothes, buy my groceries, pay my gas bill, pay my electricity and transportation costs, and then pay all my basic living expenses first? Wait…is cable a living expense?" She chuckles and slaps her knee and says, "Just kidding!" She continues, "And then after that, whatever I decide to give from my heart is OK with God?"

"That's right, Mom," I reply, "and for those middle-class and rich folk in the church, making five, six, and seven-figure incomes, they now can't get away with comfortably paying only a tenth of their income, knowing they can contribute much more."

I continue, "For example, only give $10,000 when they make $100,000 a year comfortably while knowing in their heart

Truth in Love

that they can give more. Remember what Paul said in 2 Corinthians 9:6 to Remember this: Whoever sows sparingly will also reap sparingly, and whoever sows generously will also reap generously. That means that if you give me the big piece of chicken, then the Lord will reward you with one or more big pieces of chicken down the line…look at it like a sort of first fruits offering…."

Mom looks at me with that *I wasn't born last night* look and says, "Nice try, devil, but one thing I do know is that you ain't getting my big piece of chicken! I also know that first fruits ain't the first piece of chicken either, it's the best piece of chicken and you ain't the Lawd, so I get the best piece of chicken in this here *chuch*!"

She continues, "I rebuke you from the pit of H-E-double hockey-sticks because it's better to throw a stone mill around your neck than to cause a cookie to crumble!"

We both burst into laughter and start singing as I pull off, "There is powder, powder, wonder working powder in da blood…ha, ha, haahh!" all the way home from KFC!

-$ $ $-

We now mutually enjoy our newfound freedom from the false doctrine of tithing. But like a movie scene that fades from the illusion of a dream of happiness into the nightmarish reality of heartbreak, I realize that, sadly, my

Chapter 12

mom and I will never get the chance to have this conversation.

At the young age of 57, and unnecessarily too soon, my mom died. And though it was said to be from heart problems, I believe it really was from heartbreak and financial distress.

The type of heartbreak and stress that hits you on your deathbed and makes you question everything that a so called man or woman of God has ever told you.

She may have thought, "Where is my healing, my prayer requests, my blessings, and my God, now?"

She may have even thought it was "God's will" or even that God failed her.

However, I'm sure it was not God's failure or God's will for her to be taken home, as some might presume—it was man's failure. I believe man's selfish will contributed to her death by betraying her trust with unscriptural teachings.

- $ $ $ -

There's also something called Financial Distress Disorder, similar to high blood pressure because it's also a silent killer. It can adversely affect your mental and physical well-being, impacting your bank account and your immune system.

Irresponsible tithing or giving can create anxiety, worry, stress, and a sense of scarcity. Poor management of money comes from not being able to meet your basic financial obligations. Suppose you're tithing from your gross weekly only to find yourself unable to provide for your basic needs. In that case, you are a candidate for financial stress disorder.

However, in my experience, pastors prioritize their needs over the congregant by manipulating the scriptures at their expense.

Some pastors use the excuse of saying conveniently that it's "God's Will," while it's really them imposing their will on another person for their own benefit.

Have you ever heard someone tell you, "God told me to tell you _____" (you fill in the blank), and you're like, "Well, God didn't tell me that!"

It's because He[God] didn't... your friend, teacher, or pastor did!

If you were happily married and your pastor, who's also married, came up to you and said, "God said you were going to be my wife," would you divorce your husband, or would common sense tell you that your pastor might just be Satan himself?!

Chapter 12

It is man's failure to not rightly divide the Word, and it is man's will to put less emphasis on spiritual needs, and more emphasis on material greed—and this is why they demand tithing— they use God's Name for their gain.

As a teacher, spiritual or otherwise, we are supposed to teach to bring about change; however, if people are suffering or even dying from a curriculum that doesn't show progress and keeps them spiritually and financially poor, it's time to change teachers!

Now, for you Christians who will say, "God is sovereign and if my pastor says that it's God's will to divorce my husband, who am I to disobey God?" I'd say to you, there's also a thing called free-will my sister, and just because you freely believe something, doesn't make it true!"

Truth in Love

Let's take a Pause Break. After reading my story, I am hopeful that it compels you to have the same conversation with your mom. In your own love language.

Here, I want to help you get started with my *Dear Moma Letter*. Besides, this is a private conversation between you and your mom, while you can still save her.

Below is a template letter you can use to start the conversation. Remember, you will know exactly what to say and how to say it, if you speak from your heart—as I had done in this chapter.

- -

Dear Moma,

_____

_____

_____

_____

_____

_____

_____

_____

_____

Chapter 12

Chapter 13

How a Mom Can Be Set Free, To Live Stress Free

"Then you will know the truth, and the truth will set you free."—John 8:32

And that includes free from unbiblical tithing! You can't argue with the truth. Why do you think it's so important to know the truth about anything and everything?

It's because truth sets you free from the mental imprisonment of not knowing, and releases you into the

Chapter 13

logical freedom associated with knowing—despite your ideas on morality, religion, and beliefs.

Corrupted knowledge is like a merry-go-round, and like a child that jumps off of a moving merry-go-round, once you have realized the lies that are causing you to go in circles, you'll jump off!

Some will land on their spiritual feet, some will suffer emotionally-skinned knees, and some will experience financial scars and bruises.

However, for those who are brave enough, courageous enough, and willing enough to jump off this scary go-round of false teaching and lies, you will find that you'll land on the rock-solid foundation called the Truth—and once you've landed on Truth, you won't mind standing on it alone.

- $ $ $ -

Facts are the absolute truth because facts are true for everyone. In contrast, subjective truth is based on a person's experiences, feelings, and opinions. Absolute truth is for absolutely everybody, and no one is above the truth—not even your beloved pastor.

Suppose everybody sticks their hand in hot grease. In that case, everybody's hand will get burned because that's an

Live Stress Free

absolute truth... so, likewise, if everybody gives 10% of their income over a lifetime, everybody will see themselves getting a little poorer and their pastor getting a little richer! I believe my mom learned this truth at the unnecessary expense of a shortened life span, and some of your moms are following her same path slowly through false teachings and unsound doctrine. However, this information can slow that roll to a stop and they can readjust to the normal idle speed for living a long life called "stressless."

Stress kills. Financial distress kills. If not dealt with immediately upon their symptoms, both can lead to heart disease, cancer, anger, depression, and damage to your nervous system (sometimes causing a mom to smack you for eating her Snickers bar!).

Now add the challenges of a single mom with four kids living below the poverty line. Heck, one of me as a child was enough to stress any mom out!

Now imagine the added stress of your pastor, your judgmental church family, the guest speakers, and your surroundings telling you, "You're not blessed because you don't give enough."

I mean, often my mom had to ask to have back the money she just tithed, only to get a prayer and a "No"—and every "No" slowly chipped away at her life!

Chapter 13

Isn't the church supposed to be a house of refuge and not a house of refuse?!

Now, add heartbreak to the mix. No one can sustain a life of disappointments, along with the challenges that come from constant worry, constant rejection, or constant negativity, and expect to live a long life. The body, at some point, will give in and give up just to be at peace.

It's estimated that 80% of tithers are women and this false tithing teaching doesn't have to be your mom's experience any longer. Your mom's situation also doesn't have to be identical to mine to be able to relate and sympathize with me on why you would want your mom to know this information—we can all identify with each other's pain and misery that isn't our own.

What good would this information do for your mom? Well, It would mean more money for things like quality food, important medications, necessary clothing, and valuable household items, but mostly, return her to the place we all are naturally born with, peace and freedom.

Through this well-studied information, she can now surely be set free from all of the misunderstood and corrupted knowledge taught by money-loving pastors and replace it with practical and honest truth provided by a mother-loving son, daughter, or friend.

- $ $ $ -

Lies kill whereas truth heals. This is why truth will always be a threat to beliefs because beliefs go when the truth is exposed—and that's precisely what this book does.

There's nowhere to go when you know the truth about anything except back to your comfortable corner called "what I want to believe," which is a decision to remain ignorant, inauthentic, and poor.

Now, with this information, you can choose differently.

- $ $ $ -

Suppose your friend, your family member, or your mom is tithing on income that can be used to provide a better quality of life for themselves. In that case, the information in this book could be the pivotal message in their lives if they are willing to read, study, test, and then apply it to their present lifestyle.

And maybe they wouldn't have to succumb to the slow physical and spiritual death caused by the misuse, misunderstanding, and misinterpretation of the scriptures —like my mom did.

Chapter 14

How Belief Can 'Kill' a Mom

The Pastoral Placebo Effect

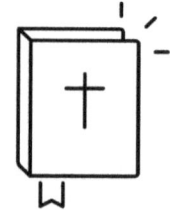

Yes, you're right; it wasn't really only tithing that killed my mom. What killed her was twofold — unscriptural tithing fortified with belief and conditioning.

You can't grow past what you don't know; belief is not knowing, whereas seeking is growing. Men have always been teased about how they never stop to ask for directions when lost and continue to drive further and further in the wrong direction.

What a Mom Believes

In contrast, if they stopped and asked for directions, they could now go and "grow" in the right direction. When we don't seek the truth, belief becomes our eternal rest stop that hinders us from arriving at our destination, called the Truth.

Therefore, the journey of belief and lies will never end because we haven't looked in our human manual and discovered why our internal check engine light is illuminating in our mental instrument panel called the "I don't know" light. It's flashing to warn you that if you keep driving on belief, you can do catastrophic damage to your physical, spiritual, and mental well-being.

The mistranslation and misinterpretation of scripture, sprinkled with poverty, poor diet, and emotional stress, can be a recipe for an early transition to the pearly gates; however, if we start investigating everything we've been told that doesn't agree with our spirit at its inception, then expose it as a lie, we can avoid the destructive conditioning that it does to the mind, our diet, and our pocketbook over time.

Belief can be a powerful placebo, and it works for positive and negative beliefs, so it behooves us all if we believe what we know, accept what we don't know, and let the Truth be the authority.

Chapter 14

A mind conditioned by falsities, lies, and propagated ideas can be critical and dangerous. From birth, we are conditioned to believe everything we're told, whether male or female, black or white, smart or dumb, and we accept them as true by an authority who was also conditioned.

Then, at some time in our lives, realities cause us to question our conditioning. We find out that it's OK to play with Johnny, even though you were told he's a different color and not to.

And that it's OK to play basketball, even though you're a girl and are not supposed to.

And that it truly is OK to listen to R&B music, even though you were told to listen to Gospel because you have to.

Or that it's OK to not give 10% of your gross paycheck to your church, even though you were told to do so or God will curse you, and you'll burn in a lake of fire, and your wig will fall off while you're testifying, and your knee caps will fall off because you don't have gluten in your diet, and, and, and…

Do you see what conditioning can do to your mind, solidified by fear, anger, hate, doubt, and lies?

At what point do we throw out the conditioning that's caused unnecessary misery in our lives? When we feel the pain caused by that conditioning the first time.

What a Mom Believes

- $ $ $ -

In sports, conditioning prepares you for whatever physical game you're about to play, whether it be baseball, basketball, football, or even weight lifting.

Do you walk up to a 100-pound dumbbell and start curling it or do you have to start with 10 pounds and work your way up? What would happen if you tried to curl the 100-pound weight without conditioning could be either breaking your wrist, tearing your bicep muscle from the bone, straining your tendon, or simply saying, *"Ouch!"* at your attempt. *Ouch* is the inherited intelligence that tells us when something isn't right physically, mentally, or spiritually.

If your personal trainer says, "You should be able to curl 100 pounds." And you know you can't because you know it's too heavy… you don't try it anyway. If your therapist says, "You should be able to get over your husband's promiscuous exploits." And you know it's causing you to have ulcers… you don't keep trying to tolerate it anyway.

And suppose your pastor is telling you to tithe on all your increase, and you know that it will cost you your basic needs for the survival of you and your family. In that case, you don't do it anyway, you say, *"Ouch!"* and pick a lighter weight, a different partner, or a different church.

Chapter 14

- $ $ $ -

Conditioning is the pain we've grown to tolerate because we've been taught to "not question" authority who's been conditioned to be in power. We accept the pastor's message as the literal interpretation of God, despite the conflict it creates in our not knowing that the conflict is a sign that something needs to be questioned, sought, and tested to be understood or discarded.

The conflict is caused by conditioning trying to usurp intelligence. Do we need to tear a muscle, develop ulcers, or lose our homes before we realize that maybe our minds have been illogically conditioned?

Can we start to question, observe, and be aware of anything that's been told to us by those we call our leaders, teachers, pastors, and prophets, and don't act upon their words because we now know that it's a form of external conditioning?

Whether internal or external, the way to end it is to stop acting on it. When we don't try to lift a weight we know is too heavy for us, continue to try and tolerate the behavior of a spouse we know is too painful for us, or continue to give money that we know we don't have, we no longer act out of a conditioned mind but of a God-given intelligence when we simply stop!

What a Mom Believes

- $ $ $ -

It's documented that patients have been told by doctors that they have a year to live, given a fake pill claiming it may reverse their illness, and through self-healing and positive belief have outlived their children—that's the placebo effect.

Then, some people were told through the negativity that they would be imprisoned before they were 21, believed it, and are now reading this book from behind bars—that's called the nocebo effect.

Why do negative and positive beliefs both work? Because they're both nurtured beliefs that appeal to our minds, are accepted, and then are manifested by our actions for self-serving reasons.

Some people use belief as a resting place in their life's journey because the fear of knowing their true destiny may be too much reality to bear. If we allow belief to quell our natural urge to seek, we may never find out the trash of lies we've collected as truth that's actually deterring us from the treasures of reality waiting for us along our life's paths.

Pastors can be a placebo or a nocebo through spiritual hexing when they teach lies as if they're the Truth. For example, if you are told that God will bless you with a check in the mail for tithing, then positive belief can make you

Chapter 14

think that your tax refund was that blessing. However, if you also are told by your pastor that not tithing 10% of your income is a curse, then you might attribute the loss of your job, home, and family to that belief.

However, if you'd investigate both of these situations, you'd discover that you had a tax refund coming regardless of your tithing, and you may have lost your job, house, and family due to the downsizing of your company. Both can be explained with investigation and by applying common sense and logic.

That's one of the fundamental problems of the human condition regarding sharing corrupted knowledge and faulty understanding—it almost always equates to poor understanding and poor translation. When you are tied to lies through religion, perception, rituals, and traditions, you miss the natural process of life, which is freedom.

If you live with the idea that 2 + 2 = 3 (which is a lie) all of your life and that's the framework you use to apply to your problems, then life will be very problematic until you discover that 2+2 is actually 4. Once you discover this, you can make the necessary adjustments and apply it everywhere in your life that truth is needed—including in relationships with your spouse, family, friends, and your pastor.

What a Mom Believes

For example, you may have to leave a job you hate and transition comfortably into a new one. Or you may have to quit one immediately, without one lined up, and suffer the consequences of that choice.

What doesn't kill you WILL make you stronger! Either way, the truth that you were unhappy with that job is all that matters, and now you are free to either enjoy your new job or find one that you love!

I'll say this again, truth is simply common sense. It doesn't take a rocket scientist to figure out what to do if your unemployment, stimulus, disability, or social security check doesn't allow you to give 10% of it to your church. Between knowledge-based intelligence (what you know) and logical intelligence (your ability to apply that knowledge), you could easily see that tithing 10% could be disastrous.

If your rent is due, your cupboards are bare, or you need money for gas to transport you and your family, then tithing the 10% will cause unnecessary hardship. That actually puts you as a recipient of the tithes, as opposed to the payer of the tithes, because the tithe goes to the needy, not the greedy.

It all comes down to the application of the natural Truth: When you don't eat, you naturally get hungry, and when you give more than what you have, you naturally will suffer.

Chapter 15

How a Mom Can See Observation, as 'Wisdom'

"If any of you lacks wisdom, you should ask God, who gives generously to all without finding fault, and it will be given to you." —James 1:5

The end of ignorance is the beginning of wisdom, and understanding is the essence of wisdom. Questions are necessary to acquire wisdom and understanding, which requires studying, so your first question after your study on

Observation vs Wisdom

tithing should be: "What scripture says that tithing went from being fruit to becoming loot?"

I can save you some time by telling you upfront that you won't find it because it doesn't exist!

Speculations, assumptions, and presumptions are not substitutes for the Truth. Just because everybody's been told to do something, and everybody is doing it, and it's how it's always been done by everybody, doesn't mean everybody is right. Everybody could be wrong!

Some traditional practices need to be challenged because some traditions are not necessarily the right way to do something—they are sometimes traditional practices because no one dares to say it's wrong and needs to be changed. Unbiblical tithing is one of those traditions.

- $ $ $ -

There's an easy way to discover this by asking yourself, "How does this tithing law operate and work in your lifestyle and everyday living?"

You'll see clearly that you don't own a field to grow produce and tend to cattle, there is no Levitical Temple or storehouse for your tithes, and there are no Levites around to sit and eat your tithes with!

That's right, I said, "Sit and eat the tithes with."

Chapter 15

People, we can't rely on a past precedent or a previous lifestyle to tell us how we are to live today because you can't apply an outdated and outmoded way of life to an upgraded and evolved way of living. I encourage you to study these two scriptures:

> "30 And all the tithe of the land, whether of the seed of the land, or of the fruit of the tree, is the Lord's: it is holy unto the Lord. 31 And if a man will at all redeem ought of his tithes, he shall add thereto the fifth part thereof. 32 And concerning the tithe of the herd, or of the flock, even of whatsoever passeth under the rod, the tenth shall be holy unto the Lord."—**Leviticus 27: 30-32 (KJV)**

> "Eat the tithe of your grain, new wine and olive oil, and the firstborn of your herds and flocks in the presence of the Lord your God at the place he will choose as a dwelling for his Name, so that you may learn to revere the Lord your God always."
> **—Deuteronomy 14:23**

Is there any confusion about the words land, seed, fruit, or flock? Is there any confusion about eating the tithe? When was the last time you sat with your pastor and equally distributed the tithing monies? Not going to happen, right?!

Do you see the obvious here? The tithes were commanded by God to be given and eaten back then, whereas today's

Observation vs Wisdom

tithes are required by the pastor to be taken and deposited on Monday morning!

Again, fruits and vegetables didn't support the temple back then because of the shekel tax, so stop trying to justify tithing today by speculating, assuming, or presuming that the tithes had to become money—because it never was.

I know it may appear redundant; however, I keep reiterating that it was never money for a purpose and that's because I want you to get it that your money belongs to you and that it is "you" that belongs to God—what greater gift could you give to God today, than to take care of yourself, with the resources, provisions, and income that's been provided for to you already?

Tithing your money under the Old Covenant is like paying your rent with fruit, it's not an acceptable or applicable medium of exchange for either God, you, or your landlord!

Isn't living healthier, exercising, and utilizing your gifts, talents and expertise to their fullest capacity giving God your best?

Is giving God your best sacrificing your child's college tuition payment out of an obsolete command to tithe from what you don't have? Could it be you making that payment

Chapter 15

because you've been provided the common sense and income to pay it, which you have, thereby ensuring that they achieve their educational goal, which will bring glory to God?

This also includes you and your child. Does giving your best to God mean tithing with money that's needed for medication, at the risk of you getting sick or would giving your best to God be that you pay for that medication so that you can prevent sickness?

Would giving your best to God deprive you of any of your fundamental needs for you and your family, food, clothes, and shelter, so those things were provided for your pastor?

I think not, according to **1 Timothy 5:8 (KJV)**, which says:

"But if any provide not for his own, and specially for those of his own house, he hath denied the faith, and is worse than an infidel."

-$ $ $-

I strongly believe that giving your best to God is giving your best to one's self first so they can give your best to others. After all, it is said we are the temple of God; therefore, by giving to ourselves first, we are also giving to God first.

Chapter 16

How a Mom Can Fast From 'tithing'

The 30-Day Tithing Fast

Just like an old diet that causes us to buy bigger belts and larger dress sizes for a new figure to arrive, we must implement a new diet to get rid of the old one. Old Testament tithing is dying, whereas New Testament giving is living—because living is giving.

Yep, you heard me right, if you're giving a tenth of what you need to live on as far as food, clothing, and shelter, then you're dying a slow death. So, I'm challenging you to a

Chapter 16

tithing fast. However, first, you must get rid of the old mindset to make room for your new mindset, or else you'll fall back into your habitual tithing instead of developing spiritual giving.

Sometimes, along with the loss of physical weight, we also need a detox of spiritual waste. Instead of fasting to lose the weight of too many Snickers bars and my favorite White Castle hamburgers, this one will be to lose the excess weight of weak and nutrient-deficient false spiritual food and misinterpreted scripture (that I like to call "flipture") so that we can gain the muscles of spiritual strength and a mighty mass of knowledge.

How is it done? Simple, I call it the 3 S's:

1. Stop tithing biblically

2. Start giving scripturally

3. Study living spiritually in order to attain a balanced mental, physical and spiritual mindset.

These three, done correctly, are the three keys to the truth that 'frees you to be' and to have your heart's desires.

Now before you call me a demon from the pit of hell, let me explain how it's done from my own experience. It may come

30-Day Tithing Fast

as a surprise; however, I noticed I was more blessed after I did these three things in every area of my life.

When tithing as instructed through indoctrination, out of fear and obligation, I often never had enough to make ends meet, which created more stress and strained my spirit.

However, when I stopped tithing and started giving of myself, my time, and my love, my life changed forever. And these are three things that everyone has to give because they're a part of our nature; therefore, it's part of what we have to give. I also discovered a few other things by sharing what I had, as opposed to what I didn't have.

- $ $ $ -

I now found that I had enough money to pay bills on time, which led to paying down debt, which freed me to give more.

I now had enough money to buy better work-related tools, which led to better-paying jobs, which freed me to give more.

I now had enough money to help family, friends and loved ones in need—which freed me to give more!

True love, to me, is unconditional giving without expectation; and giving your tithes out of obligation, for expectation of a blessing or blessings isn't "giving" to me,

Chapter 16

it's investing—like a spiritual lottery ticket. Uh-oh... it's quiet out there now! LOL!

Seriously though, some of you are already blessed beyond measure, and instead of wanting what you have, you want what you don't have.

"Lord, if you give me that new car!" You have a perfectly running car that's only a few years old—and you tithe.

"Lord, if you give me that 10-bedroom house!" The one you have is a three-bedroom, and only you and your husband are living in it—and you tithe.

"Lord, if you give me a 6-figure salary!" and you're already making a high five-figure salary, have an 850 credit score, with minimum debt—and you tithe.

Wouldn't you say these people are blessed beyond their needs, and maybe with a little shift in their perspective, they can see that they already have what they want?

How about this for perspective: the COVID-19 pandemic killed millions, thousands were left homeless in this country of God's plenty, and there was war between Ukraine and Russia, causing unimaginable hardships on families—now, how blessed are you to have survived all of that?

30-Day Tithing Fast

Now, let's reverse the previous prayers: *"Lord, if you will just give me a car!"* You're a hardworking person who catches the bus every Sunday—and tithes.

"Lord, if you just give me a house!" You're a single mom who lives in a small apartment with two kids—and you tithe.

"Lord, if you will just give me one good job!" You work a day job and a part-time night job—and you tithe.

Tell me, is it the one who wants that deserves the blessings, or is it the one who needs that deserves the blessings? Who appears to be ungrateful about what they don't have and who seems grateful for what they do have?

The difference is one prays from a shallow sense of desire, where one prays from a deep sense of need. If this is us, we need to check our hearts, recalculate our blessings, adjust our prayers, and allow the truth of current situations to be freely appreciated.

A tithing fast will show the contents of your heart by the process of eliminating who you are not whilst revealing who you are. If you are tithing your 10% <u>comfortably</u> every week, and you have a new pair of $200 Nine West pumps every Sunday, maybe you should tithe less and give more.

Chapter 16

If you are tithing your 10% <u>uncomfortably</u>, and you have to borrow money for gas to get to work and church, then maybe you should tithe less and give more.

You see, if those who can give more- give more- and those who can't -tithe less, the law of sowing and reaping will balance out everything. If that person buys one less pair of shoes and supports their church, and that one person takes that tithing money they don't have and puts it in their gas tank, not only does the church continue to be supported, but it also supports the person who now has gas to get to the church. This is how we support each other and our church—by sacrificing affluence to become more generous.

However, after reading this book, some of you might decide you no longer want to support your church… and that's ok! Then again, maybe this is an opportunity to approach your pastor in love with a few faithful and trusted members and discuss tithing. And hopefully, those who are open to their blind ignorance or misinterpretation will repent and correct their teaching (as the mega pastor Creflo Dollar has recently done), or they may digress when you ask these questions—and you can decide whether you will remain in a church that chooses money over the ministry.

Some pastors may profess to put God first until it costs them their livelihood. Either way, the truth has set both of you free!

30-Day Tithing Fast

- $ $ $ -

If you had ever experienced in your childhood playing with toys that floated in the bathtub or had an inflatable inner tube for the swimming pool, then you would probably remember that when you held down that raft or toy, it would only stay down as long as you held it down.

But when you let it go, it would float wherever it liked because it was finally free to be. This is what it means when it says that the truth will set you free because lies can only be held down for so long before it finds their way to the surface, called truth.

This realization that the truth was being suppressed got me to stop tithing and to start giving—and the fact that I had been trying to hold down in my swimming pool of reality was personal accountability.

Complaints are merely a call for action. Unfortunately, from my experience with myself, and probably with most Christians, we will complain about our lives and defer personal responsibility by saying, "Jesus take the wheel" when they already know how to drive!

Personal accountability got me to see that all my needs—food, shelter, and health—were already provided for. It was up to me to provide for the wants in my life. By taking a personal evaluation of your own life, you can see whether

Chapter 16

God is holding back the things you want to add to your life or if your own inaction is holding you back. This tithing fast will help you trim the fat off of "flipture" as well as help you gain muscle and strength in the truth!

How do I do it... this tithing fast, you ask? Well, here's a soft template that I used personally to improvise your ideas from.

WEEK ONE: You could take the first week's tithe and cook someone a casserole, or give someone a Chipotle gift card, or you could pay for the groceries for a week for someone who's family is in need.

WEEK TWO: The second week you could either provide childcare for a day or two, provide pick up or drop off services for someone whose child is in a childcare facility, or you could pay for someone's weekly childcare cost.

WEEK THREE: The third week you could buy some single moms a box of diapers, you could purchase a diaper bag, or buy a stroller off their gift list.

WEEK FOUR: That fourth week you could pick up that elderly person for errands, give them a gas card, or pay their car payment for that month up to the amount of your monthly 10%.

30-Day Tithing Fast

WEEK FIVE: And if there's a fifth week, you could write a prisoner a letter of hope, send them a book of inspiration, or give them the ultimate gift, which is your time to visit them.

The immediate blessing you'll receive (besides their smiles, joy, and tears) when that person who has been imprisoned sees someone who sees past what they've done, and sees the value in who they are, will far surpass the happiness of anything material.

Material gifts are temporary, however, spiritual gifts are forever. Are you seeing how this works? It's about doing what you can, not what you're obligated to, which is the very meaning of "as your heart purposeth"—and everybody can do something. :)

- $ $ $ -

If you do this fast correctly, then I can guarantee you that you'll be more blessed after those 30 days of not tithing under the law than you were before you fasted and were tithing under the law.

And if you claim that you're not, I want you to prove to me that it's because you didn't tithe, that you weren't blessed, to which I'll reply, "That's impossible!"

Chapter 16

How would I be able to prove that? Easily, go to your computer and type in the search "World Hunger, famines, and homelessness." You'll discover that not only 10's of thousands of children die every day from hunger, but thousands more are also suffering from malnutrition.

There are over 150,000 homeless in California and 33% are families. There are over 97,000,000 COVID-19 cases in the U.S., with over 1 million deaths.

Now, I'll ask you again, Mr. or Mrs. Tither, can you prove to me, that when you stopped tithing under the law, that you weren't blessed because you stopped tithing? Or did you simply just not get what you wanted?

I think you'll find that generosity is the greatest form of tithing and the greatest form of giving!

30-Day Tithing Fast Journal

Week 1:

_____
_____
_____

Week 2:

_____
_____
_____

Week 3:

_____
_____
_____

Week 4:

_____
_____
_____

Week 5:

_____
_____
_____

Chapter 17

How a Mom Is Honored 'With Truth'

"Honor your father and your mother, so that you may live long in the land the LORD your God is giving you."
—Exodus 20:12

There is no person on this earth that has given more spiritually to her religion than my mom, simply because she gave more than she had.

There is no person on this earth that's walked a longer road by faith than my mom because she gave more than she had.

Honor Mom with Truth

There is no person on this earth that suffered more physically and financially than my mom because she gave more than she had.

And there is no one that gave more sacrificially to the prophets, the traveling ministers, and their pastor in the form of seed offerings, first fruit offerings, and tithes more than my mom—and that's what I believed killed her.

It was because she gave more than she had, which goes against the very law of survival. If you give away your essential needs in life, then you become moribund, which is you enter a dying state and make it impossible to recover from what you've lost.

- $ $ $ -

Why do I believe this? Because we have a God-given right to feed, clothe, and provide shelter to ourselves first, otherwise the law of consequence says, "If we live at the expense of our future, then that will surely bring about an ensuing death."

But you know what, even though my mom didn't live to see that $682,000 check she was promised would arrive in her mailbox, I'm sure someday this book will save at least one life and reach the eyes and ears of serious readers serving as part of her legacy far past 682,000 people, until the end of forever.

Chapter 17

When you're on an airplane, the flight attendants demonstrate the proper procedure if there's a lack of oxygen. When the oxygen mask comes down, you put it on your face first before putting it on your child's face. Why do you put on yours first? Because you can't help anyone else if you're unconscious! You have to take care of yourself before you can care for someone else!

We must stop putting the proverbial tithing mask on our church's face first so that we can continue to breathe with the monetary oxygen that we're entitled to—that creates our own personal abundance and allows us to contribute to the abundance of others.

If you feel so inclined, then let this book be a guideline for how you should tithe and how you should give. After all, God needs you here to spread His message of faith, and when my mom arrived in Heaven way too soon, I believe God sent me a message saying, "Write the book based on your personal experience, go and take care of yourself first, then everyone else. Oh, and stay away from those Snickers bars and White Castle hamburgers—too many of those will have you *Going up to Yonder* and *Soon and Very Soon* you too will be going to meet the King."

Hmmm... now, why does that sound like something my mom would say? ;)

Chapter 18

A Guide for Guilt-Free Giving

This is what my book is about in a nutshell—the ability to give what you have, without feeling guilty, for not having more to give. If this is you, 10% of your income is no longer a command, it is a choice, and as with any endeavor in life, your best is all that's required today.

I can proudly say, that no one "out-gave" my mom because though she had nothing, she gave everything—and when you give everything, you give your best.

-$ $ $-

Chapter 18

Matthew 25: 31-40 says:

When the Son of Man comes in His glory, and all the angels with Him, He will sit on His throne in Heavenly glory. All the nations will be gathered before Him, and He will separate the people one from another as a shepherd separates the sheep from the goats. He will put the sheep on His right and the goats on His left.

Then the King will say to those on his right, 'Come, you who are blessed by my Father; take your inheritance, the kingdom prepared for you since the world's creation. For I was hungry, and you gave me something to eat, I was thirsty, and you gave me something to drink, I was a stranger, and you invited me in, I needed clothes, and you clothed me, I was sick and you looked after me, I was in prison and you came to visit me.'

Then the righteous will answer Him, 'Lord, when did we see you hungry and feed you, thirsty and give you something to drink? When did we see you as a stranger and invite you in, or needing clothes and clothed you? When did we see you sick or in prison and go to visit you?'

The King will reply, 'I tell you the truth, whatever you did for one of the least of these brothers of mine, you did for me.

Guilt-Free Giving

Look as hard as you want for it, exegete to your fill, however, you won't see, "And when I needed tithes, you tithed to your church."

Money has never equated to love, however, if you love your church so much that you have decided to give 10% of your income for the rest of your life then there is absolutely nothing wrong with that, and I'm sure your pastor will be as happy as a man who's church let out early to see the NFL playoffs!

However, if you choose not to tithe and give your best to yourself, your family, and then your church, I will bet my last White Castle cheeseburger that God won't hold back any blessings from you for doing so; after all, doesn't He own everything anyway? ;)

If, after reading this book, you are still confused as to whether or not you're obligated to give 10% of your income to your church, then I'd like you to take a long look at my book cover. It should become clear to you now that you know tithing was food and never money, simply because money isn't edible!

And it should be crystal clear why it was never food… tithing food back then was designed to fill bellies, whereas tithing money today is designed to fill bank accounts.

Chapter 18

Let's help our moms the best we can to understand this so that their days may be long, peaceful, and fruitful—and I know my mom would have liked that, too. :)

~ Moment of Reflection ~

How do you plan to spend your 10% now? Remember, it's YOUR business, YOUR decision, and YOUR faith.

_____
_____
_____
_____
_____
_____
_____
_____
_____
_____
_____
_____
_____
_____
_____
_____

Chapter 19

10 Reasons Christians Struggle With 'Tithing Guilt'

Guilt is a form of debt that Christianity has institutionalized as a virtue that keeps you "in the red, until you're dead". That being said, to be in debt is a threat to your abundance and to your independence.

And, if you're like me who was indoctrinated into Christianity, we must realize that we are deeply embedded in guilt and only the shovel of truth can loosen the foundation surrounding the stones called "lies and false

Chapter 19

doctrine" in order for us to permanently remove them from our minds.

I am a living witness to how we can permanently remove that guilt from our minds and replace it with the innocence of a virtuous heart. We cannot let go of a problem until we identify with clarity what it is, and today I can say with certainty that *when you know, the question goes*. In other words, tithing guilt be gone!

In no particular order, here are 10 reasons why Christians tithe, which keeps their spirits in some form of misery:

1) **Fear.** "I ain't trying to go to hell! Fire and brimstone is a powerful motivator!" Yet you're supposed to know that the veil has been torn, and there is no more condemnation for those who love the Lord.

2) **Tradition.** Your grandma and mom did it, so you continue the practice tithing, even though you know you're one check away from being homeless.

3) **Blind Loyalty.** You have no idea why you do, so you do it because others do it, which is the blind leading the blind, and then you wonder why you keep bumping into financial problems.

10 Reasons for Tithing Guilt

4) **Misinformation.** You were told that all Christians are supposed to tithe or you're robbing God. This false and misleading statement has caused many to tremble on payday, mainly because they don't know that Malachi wasn't talking to them.

5) **Status.** You like being a tither in good standing, especially when the pastor praises you during service yet he condemns those who aren't or simply just can't, and you start to feel like a self-righteous pharisee.

6) **Investment.** You think by tithing that your blessing will equal the amount you tithe, however, when you look at your bank account, the only increase you see is more debt.

7) **Judgment.** You don't want anybody talking about you or to be judged for not tithing by the church or your pastor. God forbid if Pastor Setback sees you aren't tithing and tells Mother Tell-it-All!

8) **The Curse.** You don't want anything blocking your blessings! God forbid any more evil befall upon you yet you notice that your non-tithing church neighbor seems to be rolling in abundance.

9) **Indoctrination.** You were instructed and taught with ideas, opinions, and beliefs that were never

Chapter 19

challenged that you obey—you continue to tithe, even though your spirit is vexed with suspicion every time you see the pastor's new Bentley.

10) **Prophe-liars.** They proclaim that "God said" and "God told me to tell you to don't stop tithing" even though you know that the God in you says, "Wait, what?! What's wrong with my ears?"

Now, would you like the number one reason Christians struggle with tithing? They don't STUDY THEIR WORD! Because, if they did, they would discover that... watch this...

TITHING WASN'T MEANT FOR CHRISTIANS!

Chapter 20

10 Steps To Be Guilt-Free From Tithing for Good

Confused, fear-driven, obligated, and gullible Christians are imprisoned behind the bars of guilt. However, the key to that cell has always been available and is right there in front of you—that key is called love, and it's right there in your Bible, waiting to free you forever!

Guilt-free giving does just that, it frees you unconditionally, which parallels with the innocence and the love of God the

Chapter 20

Giver, which is "as your heart purposes" and not "as man demands."

So are you ready to enjoy the fruits of your own labor, live a life of abundance, and at the same time support your local ministry? Well, let's go!

Here are 10 steps you can take to resolve your guilt where tithing is concerned:

1) **Study Jewish Law:** you'll find that the covenant was between the children of Israel and God, not between God and the children called "you and me."

2) **Study the context of the scriptures:** like a bridge, it connects you before and after scripture so that you know *why* it was said, *when* it was said, and *to whom* it was being said at the time.

3) **Study all verses on tithing:** when you understand Jewish law and the context of the texts, you will come to one conclusion… that tithing was food!

4) **Study the covenant between God and the children of Israel:** when you realize that you aren't one of the children of Israel or were around during the covenant of the Old Testament, you'll stop tithing obligatorily and start giving freely.

10 Steps to Guilt-Free Tithing

5) **Study Christ's sacrifice and fulfillment of the law:** when you truly understand the meaning of the cross, you will see that all laws, including tithing, were nailed to it with Him.

6) **Study the meaning of free-will giving:** when you understand that the Lord loves a cheerful giver and not a fearful giver, you will be at peace with giving what you can afford.

7) **Use your God-given common sense:** if you know that your rent is due, and tithing that 10% could get you evicted, you must trust the God-given common sense that says, "You can't afford tithes!"

8) **Find a church that practices New Testament giving:** there are churches out there that don't accept tithes and rely on free-will offerings—and are just as blessed as the tithing churches.

9) **Study "You":** ask yourself, " Why do I tithe?", "What motivates me to tithe?" and "What do I have to show for tithing"? Start journaling, and then start giving, and see if everything changes!

10) **Study, study, and study some more!** The secret to happiness is freedom and observation cultivates wisdom. So, (I'm inhaling deeply now to say this in one breath) when you know that tithing is a personal

Chapter 20

choice that an individual personally decides to give to their church, and not an obligatory command that the children of Israel had to obey during the time of the Levitical temples (that was only to be given to the tribe of Levi), and that tithing was food and never money, and that today's pastors have adopted the tithing law to make money, and that after Christ's work on the cross, the curse that Malachi spoke of was now void, and that with Jesus's Words "It is finished" ...there is no more condemnation (exhaling).

Now, you are truly free.

- $ $ $ -

NOW, if you're still in doubt and figure this is hogwash, here's something to think about—forget about Mom for a second, here are 10 ways you might be KILLING yourself if you continue tithing!

1) Supporting false doctrine by tithing money to your church.

2) Giving the tithes to someone other than a Levite, to whom the tithes belonged.

3) Creating a curse by disobeying God's Word.

10 Steps to Guilt-Free Tithing

4) Changing God's Word by falsely using scriptures for personal gain.

5) Giving money instead of food because the food was for provision.

6) Giving to receive when tithing was the law, and they gave out of obedience, not for profit.

7) Not accepting any increase as a blessing—to ask for anything more than what you need could be seen as greed.

8) Not acknowledging Christ fulfilled the law—you will perish from lack of knowledge, so studying the meaning of this is important.

9) Not using your increase to provide the food, shelter, and clothing scripture speaks of—if you choose to tithe money that God has given you to provide for you and your family's needs, then any hardship you endure is by your own doing.

10) Not respecting the significance of the crucifixion by continuing to practice the law, you disrespect Christ's sacrifice. Why would Jesus sacrifice His life only for you to continue to practice the law?

Chapter 20

Brothers, sisters, pastors, prophets, prophetesses, and moms, you've been waiting for this book and if this information moves you spiritually, then you must not ignore that new awareness that only the enlightenment of Truth can awaken.

It's that light that shows you that your imprisoned cell, which was made up of years of indoctrinated conditioning, fear, bondage, lies, stress and religious guilt is now open, and now all you have to do is walk out into your freedom, blessings, and abundance guilt-free.

Chapter 21

10 Things my Mom Never Received From Biblical Tithing

1) **The return of my father:** this was her number one request during family prayer. I would hear her heart through her voice saying, "Lord, send my husband home." She died waiting.

2) **A new home:** she wanted out of the housing projects just so she wouldn't have to worry about us getting

Chapter 21

into trouble. She died living in an apartment like the projects.

3) **A new car:** the main reason for her wanting a vehicle was so she never had to catch a cab, bus, or walk anymore. She caught rides to church until she died.

4) **To be debt free:** everything from the phone bill to the rented stereo system to hear her gospel music was in one of her children's names. Not because of lack of character, but because of a lack of funds. She died in debt.

5) **Her husband saved:** she wanted him to become a Christian and serve the Lord. Today, he has happily remarried and is a devout Jehovah's Witness. She died with that prayer on her lips.

6) **Healing:** various pastors told her that God would heal her if she tithed, and just to claim it. Tithing contributed to her staying sick because this was money she could have used for medication. She died of heart problems.

7) **Financial stability:** she wanted just enough money to provide for her kids and grandkids, pay her bills, live in a small house, and drive to church anytime she wanted. She died wanting those things.

10 Things Mom Never Received

8) **Peace of mind:** she read her Bible daily and then worried about everything from 1-8. Her last words were told to me, "I can't die, I need to be here for my grandchildren…"

9) **$682,000:** a pastor told her that if she tithed all she had, God said He would bless her 100 times for every dollar. My mother gave her settlement check of $682 and never as much as received a thank you note from that pastor, nor the promise of $682,000.

10) **Checks in the mail:** this was a common practice with the "guest pastors." I guess it's because you could never find and hold them accountable. Many checks were promised, and my mom died waiting for them.

- $ $ $ -

If anyone was to have the windows of heaven opened to pour out blessings for the amount of faith and money, she invested into the law of tithing, it was my mom. However, with every blessing she invested money into, there was never a return.

However, right now, I know she's making it rain in heaven with the wealth of her spiritual Father! It's just unfortunate that she never got to share her testimony, but I will with

Chapter 21

this book by telling her story. We are going to save 682,000 moms!

Let's try and remember the biblical story of the feeding of the 5,000 people with three loaves. Jesus knew they had no food and didn't ask for tithes, He just fed them because that was their most important need!

My mom was feeding the pastors while neglecting to feed herself, and those so-called men and women of God could have cared less. It's time to wake up, smell the false doctrine, and take action!

Chapter 22

Channel Your Pain to Take Action!

It was a must to write this book because I saw too many poor people struggling to pay their tithes and provide for their basic needs. They will give their hard-earned cash from either their paycheck, savings, pension, lawsuit, disability, or unemployment check to a church that practices Old Testament Levitical tithing—which is obsolete —and as a result, suffer spiritually because of the teaching, and financially because of the monetary fleecing!

This book is to be used as a relief for the guilt associated with compulsory, obligatory, and unscriptural tithing

Chapter 22

practices that don't do anything but financially and materially benefit these pastors.

I feel if I don't get this message that's been burning in me for over 10 years out, then I, too, could be contributing to the "lie-thing" laws practiced still up until this day—thereby allowing countless moms to suffer unnecessarily in the bondage of the Old Testament laws when the New Testament frees and teaches them to give guilt-free. They just need someone to point out how, and that's my reason for writing this book—with my mom's approval!

Pain is healing. When you are injured and suffer pain, the body's immune system immediately goes to work to repair, renew, and restore the peace it had before that injury. You can do the same thing by identifying the pain you've endured through unbiblical tithing and starting free-will, giving yourself back to mental, spiritual, and financial health.

- $ $ $ -

Putting God first is putting YOU first! Pay your rent, your car payment, your tuition, your grocery bills—all your basic needs—and then, as your heart purposeth, give to the church organization of your choice. Remember, the church is the people, not the building. ;)

Turn Pain into Action

What have you been promised that never came to fruition from tithing promises? First, make a list of all the material blessings you received.

Then, after you start guilt-free giving, make another list of all the spiritual blessings you accrued! You will discover that the tithes stop where the pastor banks, and free-will giving sends waves throughout this Universe!

Be blessed my beloveds,

Jam'all

About the Author

Jam'all Mokolo

Jam'all Mokolo was raised in the Christian church, and has over 30 years experience in the music ministry—and tithing.

He has witnessed first hand the master manipulators, the spiritual abusers, and "False Profits", who are not just "shearing the impoverished sheeple" with what he calls the "Twist-ure" and "Flip-ture", but also through conning, scamming, and stealing from the gullible rich. How? By requiring obedience to a law that is outdated and outmoded—the law of tithing—which was never money!

His goal is to hopefully help to break those mental chains that keep some in the bondage of tithing, thereby releasing them into spiritual and practical freedom of giving. Giving that's not attached to any form of fear, guilt, shame, obligation, expectation, or tradition. That kind of giving is "guilt-free" simply because free-will giving has no compensation attached to it. Tithing is about giving, not receiving.

Through Jam'all Mokolo's own experiences, he hopes someone will see themselves or their own Mom in his stories, study them fruitfully, and halt the slow killing perpetuated by many "lie-thing" pastors today.

He wants Moms to know:

"Money isn't edible, and fruit doesn't keep the lights on, so give as your heart purposeth for the right purpose, the right reasons, and the right cents."

THE END

"Every seed that is planted is not going to grow."
-Jam'all Mokolo

www.ingramcontent.com/pod-product-compliance
Lightning Source LLC
Chambersburg PA
CBHW032119090426
42743CB00007B/402